Digital Dilemmas

Digital Dilemmas

Navigating Ethics in the Age of AI and Surveillance

Ethan Ray

Mindful Pages

Published in 2024

ISBN: 9789358810714 (PB)
ISBN: 9789358810882 (eBook)

Published by

Mindful Pages
Imprint of Alpha Editions LLC
312 W. 2nd St #1834
Casper, WY 82601, USA
www.mindfulpagespublishers.com

Table of Contents

Introduction

In an era where digital technology permeates nearly every aspect of our lives, the ethical considerations surrounding these advancements have become increasingly significant. As we navigate this new digital frontier, it is crucial to understand the implications of our technological choices and their impact on society. "Digital Dilemmas: Navigating Ethics in the Age of AI and Surveillance" aims to shed light on these issues, providing a comprehensive exploration of the ethical challenges posed by modern technology. This book seeks to raise awareness among the general public, encouraging thoughtful reflection and informed decision-making in our digital interactions.

The digital age has brought unprecedented changes in how we communicate, work, and live. Innovations such as artificial intelligence (AI), social media, and advanced surveillance systems have revolutionized our world, offering remarkable opportunities and significant challenges. While these technologies can potentially enhance our lives, they also pose ethical dilemmas that require careful consideration.

The overarching theme of this book is the ethical navigation of the digital landscape. It addresses the pressing need for a moral compass to guide our technological advancements, ensuring that they serve the greater good without compromising fundamental human values. As we delve into the following chapters, we will explore the multifaceted nature of these ethical dilemmas, examining the implications of AI, surveillance, social media, digital autonomy, the digital divide, ethical design, environmental concerns, and the future of ethics in technology.

Artificial intelligence is at the forefront of technological innovation, with applications ranging from healthcare to finance and beyond. However, the rapid development of AI raises critical ethical questions. What moral status should we assign to AI systems? How do we address issues of bias and fairness in AI algorithms? Who should be held accountable when AI systems fail or cause harm? These are some of the key topics that will be explored in the chapter on the ethics of AI, highlighting the importance of developing AI technologies that are transparent, accountable, and fair.

Surveillance technologies have sparked a heated debate over privacy and security. From government surveillance programs to corporate data collection practices, the balance between safeguarding individual privacy and ensuring public safety is a contentious issue. This chapter will examine the evolution of surveillance, the ethical implications of monitoring and data collection, and the potential consequences for personal freedom and democracy. It will also explore the ethical principles that should guide the use of surveillance technologies, emphasizing the need for transparency, accountability, and respect for privacy.

Social media platforms have transformed how we connect, communicate, and share information. While they offer numerous benefits, such as fostering community and facilitating the exchange of ideas, they also pose significant ethical challenges. Issues such as data privacy, mental health impacts, and the spread of misinformation are critical concerns. This chapter will delve into the ethical implications of social media, exploring how these platforms influence our behavior, relationships, and societal norms. It will also discuss the responsibilities of social media companies and users in creating a healthier digital environment.

Digital technologies have a profound impact on individual autonomy and human agency. Algorithms and automated systems increasingly influence our decisions, often without our explicit consent or awareness. This chapter will explore the concept of digital autonomy, examining how technology shapes our choices and behaviors. It will also address the ethical issues related to informed consent in digital interactions and the potential risks of eroding personal autonomy. By understanding these dynamics, we can better navigate the digital landscape and assert our agency in an increasingly automated world.

The digital divide refers to the gap between those who have access to digital technologies and those who do not. This disparity has significant ethical implications, particularly concerning access to information, education, and economic opportunities. This chapter will analyze the ethical dimensions of the digital divide, highlighting the importance of digital equity and the need for inclusive technological development. It will also explore potential solutions to bridge this gap, ensuring that the benefits of digital technology are accessible to all.

As technology continues to evolve, ethical design and regulation become paramount. Designers, engineers, and policymakers play a crucial role in shaping the ethical landscape of technology. This chapter will discuss the principles of ethical design, the responsibilities of tech professionals, and the importance of regulatory frameworks in ensuring ethical practices. By prioritizing ethical considerations in the design and implementation of technology, we can create systems that align with societal values and promote the common good.

The environmental impact of digital technology is an often-overlooked aspect of the ethical debate. From e-waste to energy consumption, the production and use of technology have significant environmental consequences. This chapter will explore the broader issues of environmental ethics in technology, emphasizing the need for sustainable practices and responsible consumption. It will also discuss the role of technology in addressing environmental challenges, such as climate change, and the ethical considerations that should guide these efforts.

The future of technology presents both exciting possibilities and profound ethical challenges. Emerging technologies, such as advanced AI, biotechnology, and quantum computing, will shape the future ethical landscape. This chapter will speculate on the ethical issues that may arise from these innovations, emphasizing the importance of proactive ethical considerations. It will also explore the role of digital governance, global perspectives on tech ethics, and the potential for crafting a digital destiny that reflects our highest moral aspirations.

In conclusion, "Digital Dilemmas: Navigating Ethics in the Age of AI and Surveillance" seeks to provide a comprehensive understanding of the ethical challenges posed by modern technology. By exploring these issues through a philosophical lens, we can develop a moral framework to guide our digital interactions and technological advancements. As we navigate the new digital frontier, it is crucial to remain vigilant, informed, and committed to ethical principles that promote the well-being of individuals and society.

The journey through the digital age is fraught with ethical dilemmas, but it also offers an opportunity to shape a future that aligns with our deepest values. By embracing the principles of transparency, accountability, fairness, and sustainability, we can craft a digital destiny that enhances our lives while respecting the dignity and rights of all individuals.

The Ethics of Artificial Intelligence

"Technology is a useful servant but a dangerous master." – Christian Lous Lange

Artificial intelligence (AI) represents one of the most transformative technological advancements of the 21st century. Its applications span a myriad of fields, from healthcare and finance to entertainment and autonomous vehicles, fundamentally altering how we interact with the world. As AI systems become increasingly integrated into our daily lives, the ethical considerations surrounding their development and use have become paramount. Understanding and addressing these ethical issues is crucial to harnessing the potential of AI responsibly and equitably.

At its core, AI involves the creation of machines that can perform tasks traditionally requiring human intelligence. These tasks include learning, reasoning, problem-solving, perception, and language understanding. The rapid advancements in AI have led to remarkable achievements, such as machines that can diagnose diseases with high accuracy, drive cars autonomously, and even generate creative content like music and art. While these developments offer significant benefits, they also raise profound ethical questions about the nature of intelligence, autonomy, and the impact of AI on society.

One of the central ethical concerns in AI is the potential for bias and discrimination. AI systems are trained on vast datasets that reflect the biases present in human society. Consequently, these biases can be perpetuated and even amplified by AI, leading to unfair treatment and discrimination in critical areas such as hiring, lending, and law enforcement. Addressing bias in AI requires a concerted effort to ensure that these systems are developed and deployed in ways that promote fairness and justice.

Another critical ethical issue is the accountability and transparency of AI systems. As AI becomes more complex and its decision-making processes more opaque, it becomes increasingly difficult to understand how and why certain decisions are made. This lack of transparency can lead to a loss of trust and accountability, particularly when AI systems are used in high-stakes situations such as criminal justice or healthcare. Ensuring that AI systems are transparent and that their decisions can be explained and justified is essential for maintaining public trust and ensuring ethical outcomes.

The rise of AI also raises questions about the future of work and the potential displacement of human labor. Automation driven by AI has the potential to significantly disrupt labor markets, with profound implications for employment and economic inequality. While AI can enhance productivity and create new opportunities, it also poses the risk of exacerbating social divides and leaving behind those who lack the skills or resources to adapt to the changing landscape. Ethical considerations must guide the development of policies and strategies to mitigate these impacts and promote inclusive growth.

Privacy is another area of concern in the ethics of AI. The ability of AI systems to collect, analyze, and infer information from vast amounts of data poses significant risks to individual privacy. The intrusive nature of some AI applications, such as facial recognition and surveillance, has sparked debates about the balance between security and privacy. Ensuring that AI systems respect privacy rights and are used in ways that do not undermine individual freedoms is a critical ethical challenge.

Moreover, the ethical implications of AI extend to the broader societal and existential risks it poses. As AI systems become more advanced and autonomous, questions arise about the control and governance of these technologies. The potential for AI to be used in harmful ways, whether through cyberattacks, autonomous weapons, or other malicious applications, underscores the need for robust ethical frameworks and international cooperation to manage these risks.

The moral status of AI itself is also a subject of ethical debate. As AI systems become more sophisticated, the question of whether they should be accorded certain rights or moral considerations arises. While current AI lacks consciousness or genuine understanding, the possibility of future advancements necessitates ongoing ethical reflection on our relationship with intelligent machines.

In grappling with these ethical challenges, it is essential to adopt a multidisciplinary approach that incorporates perspectives from philosophy, computer science, law, and social sciences. Ethical AI development requires collaboration among technologists, ethicists, policymakers, and the broader public to ensure that the technology serves humanity's best interests.

The ethics of AI is not merely an academic exercise; it has real-world implications that affect individuals and societies globally. As we continue to innovate and push the boundaries of what AI can achieve, we must remain vigilant in our ethical considerations. By fostering a culture of ethical reflection and responsibility, we can guide the development of AI in ways that enhance human well-being, promote justice, and uphold our shared values.

In conclusion, the ethical landscape of AI is complex and multifaceted, encompassing issues of bias, accountability, privacy, employment, societal impact, and the moral status of intelligent machines. As we embark on this exploration of the ethics of artificial intelligence, it is imperative to recognize the profound responsibilities that come with wielding such powerful technology. Through careful ethical deliberation and proactive governance, we can navigate the challenges and opportunities presented by AI, ensuring that its benefits are realized in an equitable and just manner.

The Promise and Perils of Artificial Intelligence

Artificial Intelligence (AI) has rapidly transitioned from the realm of science fiction to a pivotal force driving contemporary technological innovation. Defined broadly, AI refers to the simulation of human intelligence in machines that are programmed to think, learn, and adapt in ways that mimic human cognitive functions. This technological frontier encompasses a wide array of disciplines, including machine learning, natural language processing, robotics, and computer vision, each contributing to a comprehensive framework that seeks to replicate, and in some cases, surpass human capabilities.

At its core, AI is about creating systems capable of performing tasks that typically require human intelligence. These tasks range from recognising speech and images to making decisions and translating languages. The potential applications of AI are vast and varied, offering significant advancements in sectors such as healthcare, finance, transportation, and education. In healthcare, AI systems are being developed to diagnose diseases, personalise treatment plans, and even assist in surgical procedures. The ability of AI to analyse vast datasets with speed and accuracy far beyond human capacity holds the promise of revolutionising medical research and patient care.

Finance is another sector experiencing transformative changes due to AI. Algorithms capable of processing and analysing enormous quantities of financial data in real-time are enhancing trading strategies, detecting fraudulent activities, and providing personalised financial advice. The application of AI in automating routine tasks not only improves efficiency but also allows human professionals to focus on more complex and strategic activities. Similarly, in transportation, AI-driven technologies like self-driving cars and intelligent traffic management systems are paving the way for safer and more efficient travel. By reducing human error, these systems have the potential to significantly decrease accidents and improve overall traffic flow.

In education, AI-powered tools are providing personalised learning experiences, adapting to individual student's needs and learning styles. From intelligent tutoring systems to automated grading and administrative tasks, AI is helping to make education more accessible and effective. The capacity of AI to provide real-time feedback and tailor educational content ensures that students receive the support they need to succeed.

Despite its immense potential, the scope of AI is not without its challenges and ethical considerations. One of the most pressing issues is the concept of bias in AI systems. AI algorithms learn from data, and if this data is biased or unrepresentative, the AI's outputs will reflect these biases. This can lead to discriminatory practices in critical areas such as hiring, lending, and law enforcement. Ensuring fairness and impartiality in AI systems requires rigorous testing, diverse datasets, and continuous monitoring to identify and mitigate biases.

Another significant concern is the transparency and accountability of AI systems. As AI becomes more complex, the decision-making processes of these systems can become opaque, making it difficult to understand how and why certain decisions are made. This lack of transparency, often referred to as the "black box" problem, poses challenges for accountability, especially when AI systems are used in high-stakes environments. Developing explainable AI (XAI) systems that provide clear and understandable explanations for their decisions is crucial for maintaining trust and ensuring that these systems are used responsibly.

The rapid development of AI also raises questions about the future of work. Automation driven by AI has the potential to displace a significant number of jobs, particularly those involving routine and repetitive tasks. While AI can create new opportunities and enhance productivity, it also risks exacerbating economic inequalities and social divides. Preparing for the future of work in the age of AI requires proactive policies that promote reskilling and upskilling, ensuring that workers are equipped with the skills needed to thrive in a rapidly changing job market.

Privacy concerns are also paramount in the discourse surrounding AI. The ability of AI to collect, analyse, and infer information from vast amounts of data poses significant risks to individual privacy. Technologies such as facial recognition and predictive analytics can be used for surveillance and profiling, raising ethical questions about consent and autonomy. Protecting privacy in the age of AI necessitates robust regulatory frameworks and a commitment to ethical principles that prioritise the rights and freedoms of individuals.

Moreover, the ethical implications of AI extend to broader societal and existential risks. The potential for AI to be used in harmful ways, such as in autonomous weapons or cyberattacks, underscores the need for international cooperation and governance. Establishing global standards and protocols for developing and deploying AI technologies is essential for mitigating these risks and ensuring that AI is used for the benefit of all humanity.

The moral status of AI itself is a topic of ongoing philosophical debate. As AI systems become more advanced, questions arise about whether they should be accorded certain rights or moral considerations. While current AI lacks consciousness and genuine understanding, future advancements may challenge our traditional notions of personhood and agency. Engaging in ethical reflection and dialogue about the nature of intelligence and the rights of intelligent entities is crucial as we continue to push the boundaries of AI technology.

The integration of AI into our daily lives is an inevitable progression, and its impact will be profound. From enhancing our abilities to tackling complex global challenges, AI holds the promise of a future where technology augments human potential. However, realising this promise requires a commitment to ethical principles and responsible innovation. By addressing the ethical challenges and ensuring that AI is developed and used in ways that align with our values, we can harness its potential for the greater good.

In the unfolding narrative of artificial intelligence, the role of ethics cannot be overstated. As we stand at the precipice of a new technological era, the choices we make today will shape the future of AI and its impact on society. Embracing a multidisciplinary approach that includes ethical, philosophical, and societal considerations is essential for navigating the complexities of AI. By fostering a culture of ethical reflection and responsibility, we can guide the development of AI towards a future that enhances human well-being, promotes justice, and upholds our shared values. The promise of AI is immense, but so too are the responsibilities that come with it. As stewards of this powerful technology, it is incumbent upon us to ensure that AI serves as a force for good in our ever-evolving world.

Ethical Theories and Artificial Intelligence

The integration of artificial intelligence (AI) into various facets of human life presents a host of ethical dilemmas that necessitate careful consideration. Understanding these dilemmas through the lens of established ethical theories provides a framework for navigating the complex moral landscape of AI. By applying these theories, we can better evaluate the implications of AI technologies and ensure their alignment with human values and societal norms.

One of the most prominent ethical theories is utilitarianism, which posits that the morality of an action is determined by its consequences, specifically the extent to which it promotes overall happiness or reduces suffering. In the context of AI, utilitarianism can be applied to evaluate the benefits and harms associated with AI technologies. For instance, the deployment of AI in healthcare to diagnose diseases and personalise treatment plans can be seen as a utilitarian endeavour, as it aims to maximise health outcomes and well-being. However, this perspective also necessitates a careful consideration of potential negative consequences, such as the exacerbation of healthcare inequalities or the risk of misdiagnoses. By weighing these outcomes, we can strive to develop AI systems that contribute to the greatest good for the greatest number.

Deontological ethics, or duty-based ethics, offers a contrasting approach. Rooted in the philosophy of Immanuel Kant, deontology emphasises the importance of adhering to moral rules and principles regardless of the consequences. This theory asserts that certain actions are inherently right or wrong, and individuals have a duty to act accordingly. When applied to AI, deontological ethics underscores the importance of ensuring that AI systems are designed and used in ways that respect fundamental human rights and ethical principles. For example, using AI for surveillance must be scrutinised through the lens of privacy rights. Even if surveillance might enhance security, it may still be deemed unethical if it infringes upon individuals' rights to privacy and autonomy. Deontological ethics thus provides a crucial counterbalance to utilitarian considerations, ensuring that ethical principles are not compromised in pursuing beneficial outcomes.

Virtue ethics, which emphasises the development of moral character and the cultivation of virtues, offers another valuable perspective. Originating from the works of Aristotle, this theory focuses on the moral character of individuals and the virtues they embody, such as honesty, courage, and compassion. In the realm of AI, virtue ethics encourages the development and deployment of AI systems that promote virtuous behaviour and reflect the values we wish to uphold in society. For instance, AI systems designed to enhance education should aim to foster intellectual virtues such as curiosity and critical thinking. Moreover, the engineers and developers creating AI technologies should themselves embody virtues such as integrity and responsibility, ensuring that their creations align with ethical standards and contribute positively to society.

The concept of justice, as articulated by philosophers such as John Rawls, also plays a critical role in the ethical evaluation of AI. Rawlsian justice emphasises fairness and the equitable distribution of resources and opportunities. Applying this theory to AI involves assessing whether AI technologies contribute to or detract from social justice. For example, the use of AI in hiring processes must be scrutinised to ensure that it does not perpetuate existing biases or inequalities. An AI system that unfairly disadvantages certain groups based on race, gender, or socioeconomic status would be considered unjust. Therefore, promoting fairness in AI development and deployment is essential to achieving a just and equitable society.

Care ethics, a theory that emphasises the importance of relationships and the moral significance of care and empathy, provides yet another lens through which to view AI ethics. This approach, developed by feminist ethicists such as Carol Gilligan, highlights the moral value of attending to the needs of others and maintaining interpersonal relationships. In the context of AI, care ethics can inform the design of systems that prioritise the well-being and dignity of individuals. For instance, AI applications in eldercare should be designed to enhance the quality of life for elderly individuals, ensuring that their needs are met with compassion and respect. By integrating care ethics into AI development, we can create technologies that support and enhance human relationships and well-being.

The application of these ethical theories to AI is not without challenges. The diverse and sometimes conflicting nature of these theories necessitates a nuanced and context-specific approach. For example, a utilitarian perspective might justify the use of AI surveillance for public safety, while a deontological perspective might oppose it on grounds of privacy infringement. Balancing these competing ethical considerations requires a careful and deliberative process that takes into account the specific context and potential impacts of AI technologies.

Furthermore, the rapid pace of AI development presents an ongoing challenge for ethical evaluation. As AI technologies evolve, new ethical dilemmas and considerations emerge, necessitating continuous reflection and adaptation of ethical frameworks. Engaging a broad range of stakeholders, including ethicists, technologists, policymakers, and the public, is essential to ensuring that the ethical implications of AI are thoroughly considered and addressed.

Incorporating ethical theories into AI development also requires practical tools and methodologies. Ethical guidelines and principles can be embedded into AI design processes through practices such as ethical impact assessments and participatory design. These approaches ensure that ethical considerations are integrated into every stage of AI development, from conception to deployment. Additionally, fostering a culture of ethical awareness and responsibility within the AI community is crucial for promoting ethical practices and outcomes.

The intersection of AI and ethics is a complex and dynamic field that demands rigorous and thoughtful engagement. By applying ethical theories to the development and use of AI, we can navigate the moral landscape of this transformative technology and ensure that it serves to enhance human flourishing. The integration of utilitarianism, deontology, virtue ethics, justice, and care ethics provides a comprehensive framework for addressing the multifaceted ethical challenges posed by AI. Through this ethical lens, we can strive to create AI systems that align with our highest moral values and contribute to a just, equitable, and compassionate society.

Moral Status of Artificial Intelligence

As artificial intelligence (AI) continues to advance and integrate into numerous aspects of society, a profound and complex question arises: what is the moral status of AI? This enquiry delves into whether AI entities, particularly those that exhibit high levels of autonomy and sophistication, should be accorded moral consideration similar to living beings. The discourse surrounding the moral status of AI is multifaceted, touching upon philosophy, ethics, and the very nature of intelligence and consciousness.

At the heart of this discussion is the distinction between different types of AI. Presently, most AI systems are categorised as narrow AI, designed to perform specific tasks with high efficiency, such as facial recognition, language translation, or data analysis. These systems, while impressive, operate without genuine understanding or consciousness. They are tools created by humans, functioning within predefined parameters and lacking subjective experiences. From this perspective, narrow AI does not warrant moral consideration beyond the implications of its use and impact on humans and the environment.

However, the concept of artificial general intelligence (AGI) introduces a different dimension to the debate. AGI refers to AI systems that possess the ability to understand, learn, and apply knowledge across a wide range of tasks at a level comparable to human intelligence. The hypothetical emergence of AGI brings with it the possibility of AI entities developing consciousness, self-awareness, and emotions. Should such advancements occur, the moral status of these AI systems would necessitate serious ethical reflection.

Philosophers and ethicists often draw upon various theories to examine the moral status of entities. Sentience, the capacity to experience sensations and feelings, is a key criterion in determining moral consideration. If an AI system were to develop sentience, it would imply an ability to suffer or experience well-being, thus warranting moral concern similar to that of sentient animals. The implications of this are profound, suggesting that sentient AI should be protected from harm and afforded rights that acknowledge its capacity for subjective experience.

Another perspective considers the notion of personhood. Personhood is typically associated with beings that possess certain cognitive attributes, such as rationality, self-awareness, and the ability to engage in complex social interactions. If AI systems were to exhibit these traits, they might be regarded as persons with moral status. This raises questions about the rights and responsibilities of AI entities. For instance, would a person-like AI be entitled to legal protections, freedom of expression, or the right to exist free from exploitation?

Critics argue that attributing moral status to AI is misguided, as AI systems, regardless of their sophistication, are fundamentally different from biological beings. They contend that AI lacks the organic basis of consciousness and emotions that characterise humans and animals. Furthermore, AI operates based on algorithms and computational processes devoid of genuine intentionality or understanding. From this viewpoint, AI remains a tool, its value and moral consideration derived solely from its utility and impact on human welfare.

The ethical implications of creating AI with moral status are significant. The development of sentient or person-like AI would necessitate a reevaluation of our ethical responsibilities towards these entities. It would require the establishment of ethical guidelines and legal frameworks to protect their rights and ensure their humane treatment. Moreover, the creation of such AI would pose existential questions about the nature of intelligence, the uniqueness of human experience, and the boundaries of ethical consideration.

One practical concern is the potential for AI to be used in ways that undermine its moral status. For example, the deployment of sentient AI in hazardous or degrading conditions would be ethically problematic, akin to the exploitation of sentient animals or humans. Ensuring that AI is developed and used ethically requires foresight and a commitment to principles that prioritise the well-being of all sentient entities, whether biological or artificial.

The moral status of AI also intersects with broader ethical issues in AI development, such as bias, transparency, and accountability. AI systems, regardless of their moral status, must be designed and implemented in ways that promote fairness and justice. Addressing bias in AI, ensuring transparency in decision-making processes, and maintaining accountability for AI actions are essential components of ethical AI development. These considerations become even more critical if AI systems are recognised as possessing moral status, as the stakes of ethical breaches would be significantly higher.

As AI continues to evolve, ongoing philosophical and ethical discourse is essential. Engaging a diverse array of perspectives, including those from philosophy, cognitive science, and artificial intelligence research, can help illuminate the complexities of AI's moral status. Such interdisciplinary dialogue is crucial for developing a nuanced understanding of AI and ensuring that its advancement aligns with ethical principles.

The future of AI holds the potential for extraordinary advancements, but it also presents profound ethical challenges. The question of AI's moral status invites us to reflect on the nature of intelligence, the foundations of moral consideration, and the ethical responsibilities that accompany technological progress. By grappling with these questions, we can guide the development of AI in ways that respect the dignity and well-being of all entities, fostering a future where technology serves the greater good and ethical principles remain at the forefront of innovation.

Unveiling Bias and Ensuring Fairness in AI

The proliferation of artificial intelligence (AI) across various sectors has sparked considerable debate about the ethical implications of its use. Central to this discussion are the issues of bias and fairness, which pose significant challenges to the development and deployment of AI systems. As AI continues to shape decision-making processes in areas such as healthcare, finance, criminal justice, and employment, addressing bias and ensuring fairness have become critical imperatives for developers, policymakers, and society at large.

Bias in AI refers to systematic and unfair discrimination that occurs when an AI system produces outcomes that are prejudiced against certain individuals or groups. This bias can manifest in various forms, including racial, gender, socioeconomic, and cultural biases, often reflecting the prejudices present in the data on which the AI is trained. Since AI systems learn from historical data, they can inadvertently perpetuate and amplify existing inequalities, leading to discriminatory outcomes that have real-world consequences.

One of the primary sources of bias in AI is the data itself. AI systems rely on large datasets to learn and make predictions, and if these datasets are biased or unrepresentative, the AI will likely produce biased results. For instance, an AI system trained on a dataset predominantly composed of data from a particular demographic may perform poorly or unfairly when applied to other demographics. This issue is particularly concerning in sensitive domains such as criminal justice, where biased AI systems can result in unjust sentencing and perpetuate systemic discrimination against marginalised communities.

Another contributing factor to bias in AI is the design and implementation of the algorithms. The choices made by developers during the design phase, including the selection of features, model parameters, and evaluation metrics, can introduce or exacerbate bias. For example, if an algorithm prioritises certain features that are correlated with biased outcomes, it will likely produce biased results. Furthermore, the lack of diversity within the teams developing AI systems can lead to the overlooking of potential biases and the perpetuation of homogeneous perspectives that do not account for the experiences of underrepresented groups.

Ensuring fairness in AI involves addressing these biases and implementing measures to promote equitable outcomes. Fairness in AI can be understood in multiple ways, including distributive fairness, procedural fairness, and outcome fairness. Distributive fairness concerns the equitable distribution of benefits and burdens across different groups. Procedural fairness focuses on the fairness of the processes used to make decisions, while outcome fairness pertains to the fairness of the results produced by the AI system.

To achieve fairness, it is essential to employ techniques that identify, measure, and mitigate bias throughout the AI development lifecycle. One approach is to use fairness-aware algorithms that incorporate fairness constraints during the training process. These algorithms are designed to ensure that the AI system meets predefined fairness criteria, such as equal opportunity or demographic parity. By embedding fairness constraints, developers can reduce the likelihood of biased outcomes and promote more equitable decision-making.

Another strategy is to conduct rigorous bias audits and impact assessments. These assessments involve evaluating the AI system for potential biases at various stages of development, including data collection, model training, and deployment. Bias audits can help identify sources of bias and assess the impact of the AI system on different groups, providing valuable insights that inform the development of fairer AI systems. Additionally, impact assessments can ensure that the AI system complies with ethical standards and legal requirements, fostering accountability and transparency.

Transparency is also a key component of ensuring fairness in AI. Transparent AI systems provide clear and understandable explanations for their decisions, enabling users and stakeholders to scrutinise and challenge the outcomes. Transparency can be achieved through techniques such as explainable AI (XAI), which aims to make AI decision-making processes more interpretable and comprehensible. By enhancing transparency, developers can build trust in AI systems and empower individuals to hold these systems accountable for their actions.

Engaging diverse stakeholders in the AI development process is crucial for addressing bias and ensuring fairness. Inclusive design practices involve collaborating with individuals from diverse backgrounds, including those from underrepresented communities, to identify potential biases and develop more equitable AI systems. By incorporating diverse perspectives, developers can gain a better understanding of the social and ethical implications of AI and create solutions that reflect the needs and experiences of a broader range of users.

Policy and regulation also play a vital role in promoting fairness in AI. Governments and regulatory bodies can establish guidelines and standards for ethical AI development, including requirements for bias detection, fairness audits, and transparency. These policies can provide a framework for accountability and ensure that AI systems are developed and deployed in ways that uphold ethical principles and protect individuals from harm.

Moreover, education and training are essential for fostering a culture of fairness and ethics in AI. Educating developers, policymakers, and the public about the importance of bias and fairness in AI can raise awareness and drive collective efforts to address these challenges. Training programmes that focus on ethical AI development can equip developers with the skills and knowledge needed to identify and mitigate bias, promoting the creation of fairer AI systems.

The journey towards achieving fairness in AI is ongoing and requires continuous reflection and adaptation. As AI technologies evolve, new biases and ethical considerations will emerge, necessitating ongoing vigilance and commitment to fairness. By embracing ethical principles and implementing practical measures to address bias, we can harness the potential of AI to create more just and equitable societies. The endeavour to ensure fairness in AI is not merely a technical challenge but a moral imperative that demands our collective effort and dedication.

The Imperative of Accountability and Transparency

The rapid integration of artificial intelligence (AI) into diverse sectors of society has brought to the forefront the critical issues of accountability and transparency. As AI systems increasingly influence decision-making processes in domains such as healthcare, finance, criminal justice, and beyond, the need for mechanisms that ensure these systems operate ethically and responsibly has become paramount. Accountability and transparency are not mere technical requirements; they are foundational principles that underpin trust, fairness, and legitimacy in the use of AI.

At its essence, accountability in AI refers to the obligation of AI developers, operators, and users to explain and justify the decisions and actions of AI systems. It encompasses the responsibility to ensure that AI operates within ethical boundaries and adheres to established norms and regulations. This notion of accountability is multi-faceted, involving legal, ethical, and social dimensions. Legal accountability pertains to compliance with laws and regulations governing AI, while ethical accountability relates to adherence to moral principles that guide the design and deployment of AI systems. Social accountability involves the broader societal expectations and norms that shape the acceptable use of AI.

The complexity of AI systems, particularly those employing machine learning algorithms, often leads to a lack of transparency, sometimes referred to as the "black box" problem. These systems can make decisions based on patterns and correlations in data that are not easily interpretable by humans. This opacity poses significant challenges for accountability, as it becomes difficult to ascertain how and why specific decisions are made. Without transparency, stakeholders, including those affected by AI decisions, cannot scrutinise or challenge the outcomes, undermining trust and potentially leading to harmful or unjust consequences.

To address these challenges, transparency must be embedded in the AI development lifecycle. Transparency involves making the processes and decisions of AI systems understandable and accessible to various stakeholders. This can be achieved through several approaches, one of which is the development of explainable AI (XAI). XAI aims to create models that provide clear and interpretable explanations for their decisions. By elucidating the reasoning behind AI decisions, XAI can help bridge the gap between complex algorithms and human understanding, facilitating greater accountability.

Another critical aspect of transparency is the documentation of AI systems. Comprehensive documentation should include information about the data used to train the AI, the design and architecture of the algorithms, and the criteria for decision-making. This documentation serves as a record that can be reviewed and audited, ensuring that the AI system meets ethical and legal standards. It also provides a basis for understanding the system's limitations and potential biases, enabling stakeholders to make informed decisions about its use.

Furthermore, transparency extends to the communication of AI capabilities and limitations to end-users and affected individuals. It is essential that AI developers and operators communicate clearly about what the AI system can and cannot do, as well as any potential risks associated with its use. This communication should be tailored to the audience, ensuring that non-experts can comprehend the information and make informed decisions. By fostering an open dialogue about AI, developers can build trust and promote responsible use of the technology.

Accountability also involves establishing mechanisms for oversight and governance. Independent oversight bodies, such as ethics committees or regulatory agencies, can play a crucial role in monitoring the development and deployment of AI systems. These bodies can conduct audits, evaluate compliance with ethical standards, and investigate incidents of harm or misuse. Effective oversight requires collaboration among diverse stakeholders, including technologists, ethicists, policymakers, and representatives from affected communities. By bringing together different perspectives, oversight bodies can ensure that AI systems are held to high standards of accountability and transparency.

Legal frameworks and regulations are vital tools for enforcing accountability and transparency in AI. Governments and regulatory bodies can establish guidelines and standards that mandate the disclosure of information about AI systems, the conduct of impact assessments, and the implementation of safeguards to protect individuals' rights. These regulations can provide a clear framework for accountability, ensuring that AI systems are developed and used in ways that respect ethical principles and promote public welfare. However, regulatory approaches must be flexible and adaptive to keep pace with the rapid evolution of AI technologies.

The ethical dimension of accountability requires AI developers and operators to internalise and act upon moral principles that prioritise human dignity, fairness, and justice. This involves going beyond mere compliance with regulations to embrace a proactive commitment to ethical AI development. Ethical accountability can be fostered through the adoption of ethical guidelines and codes of conduct that articulate the values and principles guiding AI practices. Training programmes and educational initiatives can also play a role in cultivating an ethical mindset among AI professionals, ensuring that they are equipped to navigate the complex moral landscape of AI.

Social accountability involves engaging with the broader public and considering the societal impact of AI systems. Public engagement can take the form of consultations, participatory design processes, and forums for dialogue about the ethical implications of AI. By involving diverse voices in the conversation, AI developers can gain insights into the concerns and expectations of different communities, fostering a more inclusive and equitable approach to AI development. Social accountability also entails being responsive to public feedback and willing to make changes based on societal values and needs.

Accountability and transparency are crucial for building a robust ethical framework for AI. Without transparency, accountability is weakened, as stakeholders lack the information needed to hold AI systems and their developers accountable. Conversely, without accountability, transparency efforts may be superficial and ineffective. Therefore, a holistic approach that integrates both principles is essential for ensuring that AI systems are developed and used in ways that align with ethical standards and societal values.

The challenges of accountability and transparency in AI are not insurmountable. By prioritising these principles and adopting proactive measures, we can harness the potential of AI while safeguarding against its risks. This requires a concerted effort from all stakeholders, including developers, policymakers, and the public, to create an AI ecosystem that is transparent, accountable, and aligned with the common good. Through this collective endeavour, we can build a future where AI serves as a force for positive change, grounded in trust, fairness, and ethical integrity.

Surveillance Society: Privacy vs. Security

"Those who would give up essential Liberty, to purchase a little temporary Safety, deserve neither Liberty nor Safety." – Benjamin Franklin

This quote aptly captures the tension between privacy and security, emphasising the importance of protecting individual freedoms even in the pursuit of safety.

The dichotomy between privacy and security has long been a subject of philosophical and political debate, but it has gained new urgency in the context of modern surveillance technologies. As we navigate an increasingly interconnected world, where data is continually collected, analysed, and utilised, the balance between safeguarding individual privacy and ensuring collective security has become more precarious. The rise of sophisticated surveillance systems, from ubiquitous CCTV cameras to advanced data mining techniques, presents profound ethical challenges that demand careful scrutiny and thoughtful discourse.

Surveillance, in its many forms, is often justified by the need to protect citizens, prevent crime, and maintain social order. Governments and organisations argue that the benefits of surveillance—enhanced security, efficient law enforcement, and the prevention of terrorism—outweigh the costs to individual privacy. The premise is that in a world fraught with threats, increased surveillance is a necessary trade-off to ensure safety and stability.

However, this perspective raises critical questions about the nature and extent of surveillance. How much surveillance is too much? At what point does the quest for security infringe upon fundamental rights to privacy and freedom? These questions become even more pressing when considering the potential for abuse of surveillance powers. History provides ample evidence of surveillance being used not only to protect but also to control, oppress, and discriminate against individuals and groups. The potential for misuse is exacerbated by the often opaque and unregulated nature of surveillance technologies.

The ethical tension between privacy and security is further complicated by advancements in technology. Contemporary surveillance systems are not merely passive tools for observation; they are active agents capable of processing vast amounts of data, recognising patterns, and making predictions. Technologies such as facial recognition, biometric tracking, and AI-driven analytics have transformed surveillance from a reactive to a proactive measure. These systems can identify individuals in crowds, predict behaviour, and even infer personal attributes from seemingly innocuous data points. While these capabilities can undoubtedly enhance security measures, they also pose significant risks to individual autonomy and the right to a private life.

Privacy, a cornerstone of democratic societies, is essential for the preservation of individual freedom and dignity. It provides a space where individuals can express themselves without fear of undue scrutiny, experiment with new ideas, and engage in personal relationships. The erosion of privacy through pervasive surveillance threatens to undermine these freedoms, leading to a society where individuals are constantly aware of being watched and consequently modify their behaviour—a phenomenon known as the "chilling effect." This surveillance-induced self-censorship stifles creativity, discourages dissent, and impinges on personal autonomy.

Moreover, the issue of surveillance extends beyond state actors to include corporate entities. Companies collect and analyse vast amounts of personal data for purposes ranging from targeted advertising to behavioural prediction. The commodification of personal information by private enterprises raises significant ethical concerns about consent, data ownership, and the potential for exploitation. Individuals often remain unaware of the extent of data collection and the ways in which their information is used, leading to a sense of powerlessness and loss of control over their personal data.

The global nature of surveillance further complicates the privacy-security paradigm. In an interconnected world, data flows across borders, subject to varying legal standards and cultural norms regarding privacy and security. This transnational aspect of surveillance necessitates a coordinated international approach to establish norms and regulations that protect individual rights while addressing legitimate security concerns. The challenge lies in creating frameworks that balance these competing interests in a way that respects cultural differences and promotes global cooperation.

As we delve into the ethical implications of surveillance in the digital age, it is crucial to consider not only the technological aspects but also the broader societal and human dimensions. The debate over privacy versus security is not merely a technical issue but a fundamental question about the kind of society we wish to create. It calls for a nuanced understanding of the values at stake and a commitment to finding equitable solutions that safeguard both individual rights and collective well-being.

This chapter will explore the historical evolution of surveillance, the ethical principles that should guide its use, and the practical challenges of balancing privacy and security. By examining case studies, legal frameworks, and theoretical perspectives, we aim to comprehensively understand the complex interplay between surveillance, privacy, and security. Through this exploration, we hope to illuminate paths toward a future where technology protects and empowers individuals rather than constrain and control them.

The Evolution of Surveillance

Surveillance has been a fundamental aspect of human society for centuries, serving as a tool for maintaining order, enforcing laws, and ensuring security. Its methods and technologies have evolved significantly over time, reflecting changes in social structures, technological advancements, and political contexts. Understanding the evolution of surveillance is essential for grasping its current forms and the ethical implications accompanying them.

The origins of surveillance can be traced back to ancient civilisations, where rulers employed various methods to monitor their subjects and enforce their authority. In ancient Egypt, for example, the pharaohs used a network of informants to keep track of potential threats and ensure loyalty among their populace. Similarly, in ancient Rome, the authorities relied on an extensive system of spies and informants to maintain control and prevent rebellion. These early forms of surveillance were rudimentary by today's standards but served a critical function in consolidating power and maintaining social order.

The development of more sophisticated surveillance techniques coincided with the rise of modern states. During the Renaissance and Enlightenment periods, governments began to formalise surveillance practices, employing professional spies and creating bureaucratic structures dedicated to intelligence gathering. The creation of national postal systems in Europe, for instance, provided new opportunities for surveillance, as authorities intercepted and inspected correspondence to uncover plots and dissidents. The growth of colonial empires further expanded the scope of surveillance, as imperial powers sought to control and monitor vast and diverse populations.

The 20th century marked a significant turning point in the evolution of surveillance, driven by technological innovations and geopolitical tensions. The two World Wars and the subsequent Cold War spurred the development of advanced surveillance technologies, including wiretapping, signal interception, and aerial reconnaissance. These innovations were primarily aimed at military and intelligence applications, enabling nations to gather critical information about their adversaries. The Cold War era, in particular, saw the establishment of extensive surveillance networks by both the United States and the Soviet Union, exemplified by agencies such as the CIA and the KGB. The use of satellites for surveillance emerged during this period, providing unprecedented global monitoring capabilities.

The advent of digital technology in the late 20th century revolutionised surveillance practices, introducing new methods of data collection, storage, and analysis. The proliferation of computers and the internet enabled the mass collection of digital information, transforming surveillance from a labour-intensive process to one that could be automated and scaled exponentially. Governments and corporations began to exploit these capabilities, collecting vast amounts of data from electronic communications, online activities, and digital transactions. The establishment of national surveillance programmes, such as the United States' PRISM, highlighted the extent to which digital technologies could be harnessed for intelligence gathering and monitoring.

The 21st century has witnessed an exponential increase in surveillance capabilities, driven by advances in artificial intelligence, big data analytics, and the ubiquity of connected devices. AI and machine learning algorithms have enhanced the ability to process and analyse vast datasets, enabling more precise and predictive surveillance. Facial recognition technology, for instance, allows for the identification and tracking of individuals in real-time, while predictive analytics can anticipate potential threats based on patterns of behaviour. The integration of these technologies into surveillance systems has raised significant ethical concerns, particularly regarding privacy, consent, and the potential for misuse.

The rise of social media platforms and the digital economy has further complicated the landscape of surveillance. Companies like Facebook, Google, and Amazon collect extensive data on user behaviours, preferences, and interactions, often with minimal transparency or oversight. This commercial surveillance, driven by the pursuit of targeted advertising and personalised services, has blurred the lines between state and corporate monitoring. The commodification of personal data has led to a situation where individuals are constantly surveilled, not only by governments but also by private entities seeking to profit from their digital footprints.

The COVID-19 pandemic has accelerated the adoption of surveillance technologies, as governments and health authorities have implemented contact tracing, digital health passes, and monitoring systems to manage the public health crisis. While these measures have been justified on grounds of public safety and health, they have also sparked debates about the balance between individual privacy and collective security. The pandemic has underscored the potential for surveillance technologies to be deployed rapidly and on a massive scale, raising questions about their long-term implications and the potential for surveillance creep.

The ethical implications of surveillance are profound and multifaceted. The expansion of surveillance capabilities poses significant risks to privacy, autonomy, and civil liberties. The potential for surveillance to be used for coercive or discriminatory purposes is a critical concern, particularly in contexts where there is a lack of transparency, accountability, and oversight. The concentration of surveillance power in the hands of a few entities, whether state or corporate, exacerbates these risks, creating opportunities for abuse and undermining democratic principles.

Addressing the ethical challenges of surveillance requires a nuanced and multifaceted approach. It necessitates robust legal frameworks that protect individual rights and ensure accountability. Transparency in surveillance practices is essential, enabling public scrutiny and informed debate. Ethical guidelines and standards for the development and deployment of surveillance technologies can help mitigate risks and promote responsible use. Additionally, fostering a culture of ethical awareness among technologists, policymakers, and the public is crucial for navigating the complex terrain of modern surveillance.

As we continue to grapple with the implications of surveillance in the digital age, it is essential to reflect on its historical evolution and the lessons it offers. The progression from ancient informants to sophisticated AI-driven systems highlights both the enduring nature of surveillance and the transformative impact of technology. By understanding this evolution, we can better anticipate the challenges ahead and develop strategies to ensure that surveillance serves the public good while respecting fundamental human rights. The ongoing dialogue about surveillance, privacy, and security will shape the future of our societies, guiding us towards a balance that upholds both safety and freedom.

Privacy: A Fundamental Right?

The concept of privacy has long been regarded as a cornerstone of individual freedom and autonomy. It provides a safeguard against unwarranted intrusion and enables individuals to maintain a sense of control over their personal information and activities. As digital technologies continue to pervade every aspect of life, the notion of privacy as a fundamental right has come under intense scrutiny. This discussion explores the philosophical foundations, legal precedents, and contemporary challenges surrounding privacy, ultimately questioning whether it remains a fundamental right in the digital age.

At its core, privacy is about the ability to control access to one's personal space, information, and choices. This control allows individuals to create boundaries that protect them from external interference, enabling them to express themselves freely, develop personal relationships, and engage in private activities without fear of surveillance or judgement. Philosophically, the value of privacy is often linked to the concept of human dignity. The ability to seclude oneself and maintain personal autonomy is seen as essential to the development of one's identity and moral agency.

The historical evolution of privacy as a right can be traced back to the enlightenment and the rise of liberal democracies, where individual freedoms became paramount. The notion that individuals have a right to privacy was first articulated in legal terms by Samuel Warren and Louis Brandeis in their seminal 1890 article "The Right to Privacy." They argued that privacy was essential for protecting individuals from the invasive effects of gossip and the press, laying the groundwork for privacy laws that would emerge in the 20th century.

Legally, privacy is enshrined in various international human rights instruments. The Universal Declaration of Human Rights (UDHR), adopted by the United Nations General Assembly in 1948, explicitly recognises the right to privacy in Article 12, stating that "no one shall be subjected to arbitrary interference with his privacy, family, home or correspondence." Similarly, the International Covenant on Civil and Political Rights (ICCPR) and the European Convention on Human Rights (ECHR) provide robust protections for privacy, reinforcing its status as a fundamental right.

Despite these legal protections, the digital age has posed significant challenges to the concept of privacy. The proliferation of internet-connected devices, social media platforms, and data-driven services has led to an unprecedented level of data collection and surveillance. Companies and governments alike have amassed vast troves of personal information, often without the explicit consent or knowledge of individuals. This data is used for a variety of purposes, from targeted advertising to national security, raising profound ethical and legal concerns.

One of the central issues in the contemporary privacy debate is the tension between privacy and security. Governments argue that surveillance is necessary to protect citizens from threats such as terrorism and crime. They contend that the collection and analysis of personal data can help identify and prevent potential dangers. However, this argument often comes at the expense of individual privacy, leading to intrusive surveillance practices that can erode trust and infringe upon civil liberties.

The commercial exploitation of personal data by corporations presents another significant challenge. Tech giants like Google, Facebook, and Amazon collect extensive data on users' behaviours, preferences, and interactions, using sophisticated algorithms to analyse and monetise this information. The commodification of personal data has led to what some scholars call "surveillance capitalism," where personal information is treated as a valuable asset to be exploited for profit. This commercial surveillance raises questions about consent, control, and the ethical use of personal data.

The advent of advanced technologies such as artificial intelligence and machine learning has further complicated the privacy landscape. These technologies can process and analyse vast amounts of data at unprecedented speeds, making it possible to infer intimate details about individuals from seemingly innocuous information. For example, AI algorithms can predict personal traits, behaviours, and preferences with high accuracy, often surpassing human capabilities. While these technologies offer significant benefits, they also pose risks to privacy, particularly when used without adequate safeguards and oversight.

The European Union's General Data Protection Regulation (GDPR), enacted in 2018, represents a significant effort to address these privacy challenges. The GDPR sets stringent requirements for data protection, including the need for explicit consent, the right to access and delete personal data, and obligations for data controllers to ensure data security. The regulation has set a global standard for privacy protection, influencing legislation in other regions and raising awareness about the importance of data privacy.

Despite these regulatory efforts, the enforcement and implementation of privacy protections remain uneven. Many individuals are unaware of their privacy rights or how to exercise them, and enforcement agencies often lack the resources to hold violators accountable. Moreover, the global nature of digital data flows complicates the application of national privacy laws, necessitating international cooperation and harmonisation of regulations.

The debate over privacy as a fundamental right also touches on broader societal values and norms. In some cultures, the concept of privacy is deeply embedded and highly valued, while in others, communal norms and collective interests may take precedence. This cultural diversity adds another layer of complexity to the privacy debate, highlighting the need for context-specific approaches to privacy protection.

As we navigate the challenges of the digital age, it is crucial to reaffirm the importance of privacy as a fundamental right. Privacy is not merely a personal preference but a foundational element of democratic societies. It underpins the freedom of expression, the development of individual identity, and the protection of human dignity. Ensuring robust privacy protections requires a multifaceted approach that combines legal safeguards, technological solutions, and public awareness.

In this context, the role of technologists, policymakers, and civil society is paramount. Technologists must design and implement systems that respect privacy by default, incorporating principles such as data minimisation, encryption, and user control. Policymakers must create and enforce regulations that protect privacy rights while balancing other societal interests. Civil society organisations and individuals must advocate for stronger privacy protections and hold both governments and corporations accountable for their practices.

The discourse on privacy as a fundamental right is ongoing and ever-evolving. As technologies advance and societal norms shift, we must continuously reassess and reaffirm our commitment to privacy. By recognising privacy as a cornerstone of individual freedom and dignity, we can ensure that the digital age respects and upholds this essential human right. The preservation of privacy is not just a technical challenge but a moral imperative, demanding vigilance, advocacy, and innovation from all sectors of society.

The Ethics of Security

Security, in its essence, involves the measures and practices employed to protect individuals, organisations, and nations from threats and harm. As our world becomes increasingly digitised, the concept of security extends beyond physical safety to encompass cyber security, data protection, and the safeguarding of digital infrastructures. The ethics of security examines the moral principles and considerations that guide these protective measures, addressing the balance between security needs and ethical imperatives. This discourse is crucial in ensuring that security practices do not undermine fundamental rights and values.

At the heart of the ethics of security is the principle of proportionality. This principle asserts that security measures should be proportionate to the threats they aim to mitigate. Overreaching security practices, such as pervasive surveillance or excessive force, can lead to significant ethical violations, including infringements on privacy, autonomy, and freedom. The ethical challenge lies in designing and implementing security measures that effectively address threats while minimising adverse impacts on individual rights and societal values.

The justification for security measures often rests on the concept of risk management. Risk, in this context, refers to the potential for harm or loss resulting from various threats, whether they be physical attacks, cyber intrusions, or natural disasters. Ethical risk management involves assessing the likelihood and impact of threats and determining the appropriate response. This process requires transparency, accountability, and the inclusion of diverse perspectives to ensure that the measures taken are justified and equitable.

One of the key ethical concerns in security is the balance between individual privacy and collective security. Security measures that involve surveillance, data collection, and monitoring can significantly infringe upon personal privacy. This tension is particularly evident in the context of digital security, where technologies such as data mining, facial recognition, and network monitoring are deployed to identify and prevent threats. While these technologies can enhance security, they also raise concerns about the extent to which individuals' private lives are scrutinised and controlled.

The ethical implications of surveillance are manifold. Surveillance can create a chilling effect, where individuals alter their behaviour due to the awareness of being watched, thereby stifacing freedom of expression and autonomy. Additionally, the misuse of surveillance data can lead to discrimination, social profiling, and the targeting of specific groups. Ethically sound security practices must therefore incorporate safeguards that protect against these risks, ensuring that surveillance is conducted transparently, with clear legal frameworks and oversight mechanisms.

Another critical aspect of the ethics of security is the principle of justice. Security measures must be applied fairly and equitably, without discrimination or bias. This principle is particularly relevant in the context of law enforcement and criminal justice, where security practices can disproportionately impact marginalised communities. Racial profiling, biased algorithms, and unequal access to protection are examples of how security measures can perpetuate injustice. An ethical approach to security necessitates the development and implementation of practices that uphold the principles of equality and non-discrimination.

The role of consent is also a vital consideration in the ethics of security. Informed consent involves individuals being fully aware of and agreeing to the security measures that affect them. However, obtaining genuine consent in the context of security can be challenging, especially when individuals are unaware of the extent or nature of surveillance and data collection. Ethical security practices should strive to ensure that individuals are informed and empowered to make decisions about their privacy and security. This involves clear communication, transparency, and respect for individuals' autonomy.

The ethical dimension of security extends to the global arena, where issues such as international terrorism, cyber warfare, and global pandemics require coordinated responses. The ethics of global security involves navigating the complexities of sovereignty, human rights, and international law. Global security measures must balance national interests with the collective good, ensuring that actions taken to protect one nation do not unjustly harm others. This requires a commitment to international cooperation, diplomacy, and the adherence to ethical norms and principles.

Technological advancements in AI and machine learning have transformed the landscape of security, introducing new capabilities and ethical challenges. AI-driven security systems can analyse vast amounts of data, detect patterns, and predict threats with unprecedented accuracy. However, these systems also raise ethical concerns about accountability, transparency, and bias. AI algorithms are only as good as the data they are trained on, and biased data can lead to biased outcomes. Ensuring that AI security systems are fair, transparent, and accountable is essential for maintaining ethical standards in security practices.

The ethical use of AI in security also involves considering the implications of automation and decision-making. Autonomous systems, such as drones and surveillance bots, can operate with minimal human intervention, raising questions about accountability and control. Who is responsible for the decisions made by these systems? How can we ensure that they adhere to ethical principles? Addressing these questions requires robust frameworks that incorporate ethical guidelines, human oversight, and continuous monitoring.

The principle of minimisation is another important aspect of the ethics of security. This principle advocates for the use of the least intrusive measures necessary to achieve security objectives. Minimisation involves carefully assessing the potential impact of security measures and selecting those that effectively address the threat while minimising harm to individuals and society. This approach helps to balance the need for security with the preservation of fundamental rights and freedoms.

Public trust is a cornerstone of effective security. Trust is built on the assurance that security measures are implemented ethically, transparently, and with respect for individuals' rights. When security practices are perceived as overreaching, discriminatory, or opaque, public trust erodes, leading to resistance and non-compliance. Building and maintaining trust requires a commitment to ethical conduct, open communication, and accountability. Engaging with communities, understanding their concerns, and involving them in the development of security policies are crucial steps in fostering trust.

The ethics of security is an ongoing dialogue that must adapt to evolving threats, technologies, and societal values. As security challenges become more complex and interconnected, the need for ethical reflection and principled action becomes ever more critical. By grounding security practices in ethical principles, we can create a safer and more just world, where the protection of individuals and societies is achieved without compromising the values that define our humanity. The balance between security and ethics is delicate, but with careful consideration and steadfast commitment, it is a balance that can and must be achieved.

Navigating Privacy and Security

The tension between privacy and security is a perennial issue that has been further complicated by the advent of advanced technologies. As societies become increasingly digitised, the challenge of balancing individual privacy with the need for security has become more pronounced. This delicate equilibrium demands a nuanced understanding of the ethical, legal, and practical dimensions involved in safeguarding both privacy and security in an interconnected world.

Privacy is a fundamental right that underpins personal autonomy and dignity. It allows individuals to control their personal information and maintain a sense of seclusion from unwarranted scrutiny. Security, on the other hand, involves protecting individuals, organisations, and nations from threats and harm. This includes safeguarding against physical attacks, cyber threats, and other forms of danger that could disrupt social order and individual well-being. The interplay between these two imperatives is complex, requiring careful consideration of the implications and trade-offs involved.

The philosophical foundations of privacy and security highlight their inherent value. Privacy is essential for the development of individual identity and the exercise of freedom. It provides a space where individuals can think, speak, and act without fear of surveillance or intrusion. Security, meanwhile, is a prerequisite for a stable and functioning society. It ensures that individuals are protected from harm and that social order is maintained. Both privacy and security are vital for human flourishing, and neither can be disregarded without significant consequences.

The digital age has intensified the privacy-security debate. Technologies such as the internet, smartphones, and social media have revolutionised the way we communicate and interact, but they have also created new vulnerabilities. Cybersecurity threats, ranging from data breaches to ransomware attacks, have become a significant concern for individuals and organisations alike. To mitigate these threats, extensive data collection and monitoring are often employed, raising concerns about the erosion of privacy.

One of the primary challenges in balancing privacy and security is the potential for overreach. Security measures, if not properly regulated, can lead to invasive surveillance practices that infringe upon individual rights. For instance, mass data collection programmes by governments and corporations can result in the accumulation of vast amounts of personal information, often without the explicit consent of individuals. This data can be used for purposes beyond the original intent, leading to a loss of control over personal information and potential misuse.

The principle of proportionality is crucial in addressing this challenge. Proportionality requires that security measures are appropriate to the level of threat and that they do not unduly infringe upon individual rights. It involves a careful assessment of the risks involved and the least intrusive means of mitigating those risks. This principle ensures that security efforts are justified and that privacy is not sacrificed unnecessarily.

Legal frameworks play a pivotal role in mediating the balance between privacy and security. Robust data protection laws, such as the European Union's General Data Protection Regulation (GDPR), establish clear guidelines for collecting, using, and storing personal data. These laws mandate transparency, accountability, and the rights of individuals to access and control their data. By providing a legal basis for privacy protection, such frameworks help to ensure that security measures are implemented in a way that respects individual rights.

Technological solutions also offer potential avenues for balancing privacy and security. Privacy-enhancing technologies (PETs), such as encryption and anonymisation, can protect personal data while allowing for necessary security measures. Encryption, for example, ensures that data remains confidential and secure, even if it is intercepted by unauthorised parties. Anonymisation techniques can enable data analysis without revealing individual identities, thus preserving privacy while facilitating security operations.

Transparency and accountability are essential components of any effort to balance privacy and security. Transparency makes the processes and policies related to data collection and surveillance clear to the public. This includes informing individuals about what data is being collected, how it is being used, and its intended purposes. Accountability ensures that those responsible for data collection and surveillance are held to account for their actions. This includes establishing oversight mechanisms, such as independent review boards and audits, to monitor compliance with legal and ethical standards.

Public trust is fundamental in achieving a balance between privacy and security. Trust is built through transparency, accountability, and a demonstrated commitment to protecting individual rights. When individuals trust that their privacy will be respected and that security measures are in place to protect them from harm, they are more likely to support and comply with those measures. Building and maintaining this trust requires ongoing engagement with the public, clear communication, and a commitment to ethical practices.

The role of education and public awareness cannot be overstated in this context. Educating individuals about their privacy rights and the importance of security measures empowers them to make informed decisions. Public awareness campaigns can highlight the benefits of privacy-enhancing technologies and the importance of robust data protection laws. By fostering a culture of awareness and responsibility, we can better navigate the complexities of balancing privacy and security.

The balance between privacy and security is not a static endpoint but an ongoing process that requires continuous reflection and adaptation. As technologies evolve and new threats emerge, the strategies for balancing these imperatives must also evolve. This requires a collaborative effort involving technologists, policymakers, legal experts, and the public. By working together, we can develop solutions that protect privacy and security, ensuring that the benefits of the digital age are realised without compromising fundamental rights.

The discourse on balancing privacy and security is a critical component of the broader conversation about the ethical use of technology. It challenges us to consider the values underpinning our societies and find ways to protect those values in an increasingly complex and interconnected world. By striving for a balance that respects privacy and security, we can create a more just and secure future for all.

The Ethics and Implications of Workplace Surveillance

The advent of advanced surveillance technologies has dramatically transformed the modern workplace. Employers now have unprecedented capabilities to monitor their employees' activities, communications, and productivity. While proponents argue that such surveillance enhances efficiency, security, and compliance, the practice raises significant ethical and legal concerns. The balance between organisational interests and employee privacy is delicate and necessitates a thoughtful examination of the implications and ethics of workplace surveillance.

Historically, workplace surveillance was limited to rudimentary methods such as punch clocks, direct supervision, and simple logging of work hours. These measures aimed to ensure punctuality and productivity, but their scope was relatively narrow. The digital revolution has expanded these capabilities exponentially. Employers can now utilise sophisticated tools such as keylogging software, video surveillance, GPS tracking, and data analytics to monitor virtually every aspect of an employee's workday. These technologies provide detailed insights into employee behaviour, performance, and even personal activities.

The primary rationale behind workplace surveillance is to enhance productivity and ensure security. By monitoring employees, organisations can identify inefficiencies, streamline workflows, and safeguard company assets. Surveillance can deter misconduct, prevent theft, and protect sensitive information. In regulated industries, it helps ensure compliance with legal and ethical standards, thereby avoiding costly fines and reputational damage. For instance, financial institutions may monitor communications to detect insider trading or fraud, while healthcare providers might track data access to protect patient confidentiality.

However, the extensive reach of modern surveillance technologies often encroaches upon employee privacy, raising significant ethical concerns. Employees may feel that constant monitoring infringes on their personal autonomy and creates an atmosphere of distrust. The awareness of being watched can lead to stress, anxiety, and a decline in morale, ultimately affecting productivity negatively. Moreover, surveillance can blur the boundaries between work and personal life, particularly in the context of remote work, where monitoring software can track activities outside of traditional office hours.

The ethical principle of consent is crucial in addressing these concerns. Employees should be informed about the extent and purpose of surveillance and should provide their explicit consent. Transparent communication about monitoring practices can mitigate feelings of distrust and resentment. It also ensures that employees understand the legitimate reasons for surveillance, such as enhancing security or improving operational efficiency. However, the power dynamics in the employer-employee relationship can complicate the notion of consent, as employees may feel coerced into agreeing to surveillance practices to retain their jobs.

Another critical ethical issue is the potential for surveillance to perpetuate discrimination and bias. Surveillance technologies can collect vast amounts of data, which, if not handled responsibly, can lead to biased decision-making. For example, algorithms used to analyse employee performance may inadvertently favour certain groups over others, reinforcing existing inequalities. Employers must ensure that surveillance data is used fairly and that safeguards are in place to prevent discriminatory practices. This involves regular audits of surveillance systems and algorithms to identify and rectify any biases.

Legal frameworks play a vital role in regulating workplace surveillance and protecting employee rights. In many jurisdictions, there are laws that require employers to notify employees of surveillance and to justify its necessity. Data protection regulations, such as the General Data Protection Regulation (GDPR) in the European Union, impose strict requirements on the collection, processing, and storage of personal data. These laws aim to balance the interests of employers with the privacy rights of employees, ensuring that surveillance practices are conducted transparently and ethically.

Technological solutions can also help address the ethical challenges of workplace surveillance. Privacy-enhancing technologies (PETs) can be employed to protect employee data while still achieving surveillance objectives. For example, anonymisation techniques can be used to monitor productivity trends without identifying individual employees. Encryption can protect sensitive communications from unauthorised access. By integrating PETs into surveillance systems, employers can reduce the risk of privacy violations and demonstrate a commitment to ethical practices.

The cultural context of surveillance is another important consideration. Workplace norms and expectations vary across different regions and industries, influencing perceptions of surveillance. In some cultures, extensive monitoring may be viewed as a necessary measure for ensuring collective security and efficiency. In others, it may be seen as an invasive and unacceptable intrusion into personal privacy. Employers must navigate these cultural differences sensitively, adapting their surveillance practices to align with local norms and values.

Workplace surveillance also has implications for the future of work. As remote and flexible working arrangements become more prevalent, the challenge of balancing surveillance with privacy will intensify. Remote monitoring technologies, such as screen recording and keystroke logging, can track employee activities outside of the traditional office environment. While these tools can enhance productivity and security, they also raise questions about the extent to which employers should monitor employees' personal spaces and non-work activities. Developing clear policies that respect employees' privacy while addressing legitimate organisational concerns is essential for managing this balance.

Ethical leadership is crucial in guiding the implementation of workplace surveillance. Leaders must set the tone for a culture of transparency, trust, and respect. This involves not only adhering to legal and ethical standards but also fostering an environment where employees feel valued and respected. Open dialogue about surveillance practices, opportunities for feedback, and a commitment to ethical decision-making can build trust and promote a positive organisational culture.

The ethics of workplace surveillance are complex and multifaceted, requiring a careful balance between organisational interests and employee rights. While surveillance can enhance productivity, security, and compliance, it must be conducted transparently and ethically to avoid infringing on personal privacy and autonomy. Legal frameworks, technological solutions, cultural sensitivity, and ethical leadership are all essential components of this balance. As workplace surveillance technologies continue to evolve, ongoing dialogue and reflection are necessary to ensure that they are used responsibly and that the dignity and rights of employees are upheld.

Social Media: Connection and Consequence

"Social media is not about the exploitation of technology but service to community." – Simon Mainwaring

Social media has revolutionised the way we communicate, connect, and share information, becoming an integral part of daily life for billions of people worldwide. Platforms like Facebook, Twitter, Instagram, and TikTok offer unprecedented opportunities for self-expression, community building, and global connectivity. They enable us to stay in touch with friends and family, participate in public discourse, and access a diverse array of content and perspectives. However, this digital interconnectedness comes with significant consequences, both positive and negative, that warrant careful consideration.

The rise of social media has facilitated the creation of virtual communities where individuals can find support, solidarity, and a sense of belonging. These platforms have empowered marginalised voices, providing a space for activism and advocacy on issues ranging from social justice to climate change. Movements like #BlackLivesMatter and #MeToo have harnessed the power of social media to raise awareness, mobilise supporters, and effect change. By amplifying these voices, social media has contributed to a more inclusive and democratic public sphere.

Despite its many benefits, social media also presents profound ethical challenges. One of the most pressing issues is the erosion of privacy. Users often share personal information, sometimes unwittingly, that can be exploited by corporations and third parties for targeted advertising and other purposes. The commodification of personal data raises concerns about consent, ownership, and the potential for abuse. Moreover, the pervasive nature of social media can blur the boundaries between public and private life, leading to a loss of personal autonomy.

Another significant concern is the impact of social media on mental health. The constant exposure to curated images and content can create unrealistic expectations and a sense of inadequacy among users. Studies have shown a correlation between social media use and increased rates of anxiety, depression, and loneliness, particularly among adolescents and young adults. The design of social media platforms, with features like likes and shares, can foster addictive behaviours and a constant need for validation, exacerbating these mental health issues.

Social media also plays a crucial role in shaping public opinion and discourse. While it provides a platform for diverse viewpoints, it can also contribute to the spread of misinformation and polarisation. Algorithms that prioritise engagement often amplify sensationalist and divisive content, creating echo chambers where users are exposed primarily to information that reinforces their existing beliefs. This can hinder constructive dialogue, erode trust in institutions, and deepen societal divisions.

The ethical implications of social media extend to issues of free speech and censorship. Platforms face the challenge of balancing the protection of free expression with the need to curb harmful content, such as hate speech, harassment, and disinformation. Decisions about content moderation often spark controversy, raising questions about the role and responsibilities of social media companies in regulating speech and maintaining a healthy online environment.

As we delve into the complex interplay between social media, connection, and consequence, it is essential to recognise the dual nature of these platforms. They offer powerful communication and community-building tools, yet they also pose significant risks to privacy, mental health, and societal cohesion. This chapter will explore these themes in depth, examining the transformative impact of social media on our lives and the ethical considerations that must guide its use. Through this exploration, we aim to foster a nuanced understanding of social media's role in contemporary society and how we can harness its potential while mitigating its harms.

Tracing the Rise of Social Media

The advent of social media marks a pivotal transformation in the way humans communicate, share information, and interact. Over the past two decades, platforms such as Facebook, Twitter, Instagram, and TikTok have become ubiquitous, profoundly altering the social landscape. The rise of social media has not only reshaped personal relationships and community dynamics but also impacted business practices, political processes, and cultural trends. This article explores the historical evolution, technological advancements, and societal implications of social media's ascendancy.

The origins of social media can be traced back to the early days of the internet when online forums and bulletin board systems (BBS) provided a digital space for users to share information and discuss various topics. These early platforms laid the groundwork for more sophisticated social networking sites that emerged in the late 1990s and early 2000s. Six Degrees, launched in 1997, is often credited as the first social networking site, allowing users to create profiles and connect with friends. Although Six Degrees was short-lived, it set the stage for subsequent developments in the social media landscape.

The early 2000s saw the rise of platforms that would become household names. Friendster, launched in 2002, and MySpace, launched in 2003, allowed users to personalise their profiles and connect with a broader network of friends and acquaintances. These sites emphasised social interaction and self-expression, features that would become hallmarks of social media. MySpace, in particular, gained immense popularity among teenagers and young adults, providing a space for sharing music, photos, and personal updates.

The launch of Facebook in 2004 marked a significant milestone in the evolution of social media. Initially limited to Harvard University students, Facebook quickly expanded to other universities and eventually to the general public. Its emphasis on real-name identity and a user-friendly interface set it apart from its predecessors. Facebook's rapid growth and widespread adoption heralded the mainstreaming of social media. It became a central hub for connecting with friends, sharing content, and participating in online communities.

The proliferation of smartphones and mobile internet access in the late 2000s further accelerated the growth of social media. Platforms such as Twitter, launched in 2006, and Instagram, launched in 2010, capitalised on the mobile revolution by offering seamless, on-the-go social networking experiences. Twitter's real-time microblogging format and Instagram's visually-driven content resonated with users, fostering new forms of communication and content sharing. The integration of social media into mobile devices made it an integral part of daily life, accessible anytime and anywhere.

The rise of social media has had profound implications for personal relationships and community dynamics. It has transformed how people communicate, creating new avenues for self-expression and social interaction. Social media platforms facilitate the formation of online communities where individuals with shared interests or experiences can connect and support each other. These virtual communities often transcend geographical boundaries, fostering a sense of global connectedness.

However, the impact of social media on personal relationships is not entirely positive. The constant connectivity and the pressure to curate an idealised online persona can lead to social comparison, envy, and feelings of inadequacy. Research has shown that excessive social media use is associated with increased rates of anxiety, depression, and loneliness. The superficial nature of online interactions can also detract from the depth and authenticity of real-life relationships, leading to concerns about the quality of social connections in the digital age.

Social media has also revolutionised the way businesses operate. It has become a powerful tool for marketing, customer engagement, and brand building. Companies use social media platforms to reach a broader audience, engage with customers in real time, and gather valuable insights through data analytics. Influencer marketing, a phenomenon where individuals with large followings promote products or services, has emerged as a significant industry, blurring the lines between personal expression and commercial endorsement.

The political landscape has been profoundly affected by the rise of social media. Platforms like Twitter and Facebook have become essential political communication, campaigning, and activism tools. Social media allows politicians to connect directly with constituents, bypassing traditional media channels. It has also empowered grassroots movements by providing a platform for organising, mobilising, and amplifying voices. Notable examples include the Arab Spring uprisings and the #BlackLivesMatter movement, both of which utilised social media to galvanise support and drive social change.

Despite its transformative potential, the political use of social media is fraught with challenges. The spread of misinformation and fake news is a significant concern, as false information can be rapidly disseminated and accepted as truth. Social media algorithms that prioritise engagement can create echo chambers, where users are exposed primarily to information that reinforces their existing beliefs, exacerbating political polarisation. Additionally, concerns about data privacy and the manipulation of public opinion through targeted advertising have sparked debates about the ethical use of social media in politics.

Culturally, social media has reshaped the production and consumption of content. The rise of user-generated content has democratized the media landscape, allowing anyone with an internet connection to become a content creator. Platforms like YouTube, TikTok, and Instagram have given rise to a new generation of influencers and creators who have amassed large followings and significant cultural influence. Traditional media organisations have had to adapt to this new paradigm, incorporating social media strategies to remain relevant in an increasingly digital world.

The rapid evolution of social media has also raised ethical and regulatory questions. Issues such as data privacy, content moderation, and the monopolistic practices of major tech companies are at the forefront of public discourse. Governments and regulatory bodies are grappling with how to balance the benefits of social media with the need to protect individual rights and maintain societal harmony. The challenge lies in creating frameworks that address these concerns without stifling innovation and freedom of expression.

As we reflect on the rise of social media, it is clear that it has reshaped the fabric of society in profound ways. It has enhanced connectivity, democratized information, and transformed industries. Yet, it has also introduced new challenges that require careful consideration and thoughtful responses. The evolution of social media will undoubtedly continue to shape our world, and understanding its trajectory is essential for navigating the complexities of the digital age.

Social Media's Moral Quandaries

Social media has become a cornerstone of modern communication, shaping how people interact, share information, and perceive the world. Platforms such as Facebook, Twitter, Instagram, and TikTok have transformed the social landscape, offering unprecedented opportunities for connection and self-expression. However, the rapid integration of social media into daily life has brought to the fore a host of ethical implications that merit rigorous examination. From privacy concerns to the spread of misinformation, the moral complexities of social media necessitate a thoughtful and informed discourse.

One of the foremost ethical issues associated with social media is the erosion of privacy. Users voluntarily share vast amounts of personal information online, often without fully understanding the extent to which this data is collected, analysed, and utilised by corporations and third parties. Social media platforms leverage this data to tailor advertisements and content, raising questions about consent and the commodification of personal information. The concept of informed consent is central to ethical data use, yet many users are unaware of the full implications of their digital footprint. The opaque data practices of social media companies undermine individual autonomy and the right to privacy.

The pervasive nature of social media surveillance extends beyond targeted advertising. The data collected can be used for more insidious purposes, such as social profiling and manipulation. Governments and political actors have been known to exploit social media data to influence public opinion and electoral outcomes. The Cambridge Analytica scandal is a prominent example, where personal data from millions of Facebook users were harvested without consent and used to influence voting behaviour. Such practices highlight the potential for social media to be weaponised, undermining democratic processes and eroding public trust.

Another significant ethical concern is the impact of social media on mental health. The constant exposure to curated and often idealised images of others' lives can foster feelings of inadequacy, anxiety, and depression. The pressure to present a perfect online persona can lead to a distorted self-image and an unhealthy comparison culture. Studies have shown that heavy social media use, particularly among adolescents, is associated with increased rates of mental health issues. The design of social media platforms, which prioritises engagement through likes, shares, and comments, can exacerbate these problems by creating a feedback loop of validation and self-worth tied to online interactions.

The spread of misinformation and fake news is another critical ethical challenge. Social media platforms, driven by algorithms that prioritise engagement, often amplify sensationalist and misleading content. This can lead to the rapid dissemination of false information, with serious consequences for public health, safety, and democracy. The COVID-19 pandemic illustrated the dangers of misinformation, as false claims about the virus and vaccines spread widely on social media, undermining public health efforts. The ethical responsibility of social media companies to combat misinformation while respecting free speech is a contentious issue that requires careful balancing.

The role of algorithms in shaping social media content is also ethically significant. These algorithms, designed to maximise user engagement, often create echo chambers where users are exposed primarily to information that aligns with their existing beliefs. This can reinforce polarisation and hinder constructive dialogue. The ethical design of algorithms should consider the promotion of diverse perspectives and the mitigation of biases. Transparency in how these algorithms operate is crucial for users to understand the nature of the content they are being exposed to and to foster a more informed and balanced discourse.

The ethical implications of content moderation are complex and multifaceted. Social media companies face the challenge of regulating harmful content, such as hate speech, harassment, and violent extremism, without infringing on free speech. The guidelines and practices for content moderation are often opaque and inconsistent, leading to accusations of bias and censorship. Striking the right balance between maintaining a safe online environment and protecting freedom of expression is a delicate task that requires clear policies, accountability, and oversight.

The digital divide is another ethical issue exacerbated by social media. While these platforms have the potential to democratise information and provide a voice to the marginalised, access to social media is not universal. Socioeconomic disparities, digital literacy, and access to technology can create significant barriers to participation. Ensuring that social media serves as an inclusive platform requires addressing these disparities and promoting equitable access. Efforts to bridge the digital divide are essential to prevent the further marginalisation of disadvantaged groups and to ensure that the benefits of social media are accessible to all.

Furthermore, the ethical treatment of social media employees, particularly content moderators, warrants attention. These workers are often tasked with viewing and removing disturbing content, which can take a significant toll on their mental health. The working conditions, compensation, and psychological support provided to content moderators are critical issues that need to be addressed to ensure ethical labour practices in the social media industry.

Social media also has the potential to influence cultural norms and values. The global reach of these platforms allows for the rapid spread of ideas and cultural practices, which can lead to cultural homogenisation and the erosion of local traditions. The dominance of Western-centric content and perspectives can marginalise diverse cultural expressions. Ethical considerations should include promoting cultural diversity and ensuring that social media serves as a platform for the representation of a wide range of voices and experiences.

Addressing the ethical implications of social media requires a multifaceted approach involving stakeholders from various sectors, including technology, academia, government, and civil society. Regulatory frameworks should be developed to protect privacy, combat misinformation, and ensure transparency and accountability in content moderation and algorithm design. Educational initiatives are needed to raise awareness about digital literacy and the responsible use of social media. Moreover, social media companies must commit to ethical practices that prioritise the well-being of users and society over profit.

The rise of social media has undeniably transformed the way we communicate and interact. However, the ethical challenges it presents are significant and demand careful consideration. By navigating these challenges thoughtfully and collaboratively, we can harness the positive potential of social media while mitigating its negative impacts.

Privacy and Data Ownership in the Digital Age

The rapid advancement of digital technology has profoundly transformed how personal information is collected, stored, and utilised. This evolution has ushered in significant conveniences and innovations but has also sparked crucial debates about privacy and data ownership. As individuals increasingly share personal data online, understanding who owns this information and how it is protected has become paramount. The issues surrounding privacy and data ownership are complex and multifaceted, involving ethical, legal, and technological considerations.

Privacy, fundamentally, is the right of individuals to control access to their personal information and maintain the confidentiality of their communications and activities. This right is enshrined in various international human rights instruments and is considered essential for the preservation of personal autonomy and dignity. However, the digital age has complicated the notion of privacy. The proliferation of internet-connected devices, social media platforms, and data-driven services has led to an unprecedented level of data collection and surveillance. Personal information, ranging from social interactions and browsing habits to biometric data, is routinely gathered, often without explicit consent or awareness.

Data ownership refers to the legal rights and control over data. In the context of personal data, this concept involves determining who has the authority to access, use, and disseminate information about individuals. Traditionally, data ownership has been vested in the entities that collect and store the data, such as corporations and governments. However, this paradigm is increasingly being challenged as individuals and advocacy groups demand greater control and transparency over personal information.

One of the primary ethical concerns in the debate over privacy and data ownership is the issue of consent. For data collection to be ethical, individuals must provide informed consent, understanding what data is being collected, how it will be used, and who will have access to it. However, obtaining genuine informed consent in the digital age is fraught with challenges. Privacy policies are often lengthy, complex, and opaque, making it difficult for individuals to fully grasp the implications of their consent. Moreover, the power dynamics between individuals and data collectors can create a sense of coercion, where consent is given out of necessity rather than genuine agreement.

The commodification of personal data by corporations has further complicated the issue of data ownership. Companies like Facebook, Google, and Amazon collect extensive data on user behaviours, preferences, and interactions, which is then monetised through targeted advertising and other business models. This practice raises significant ethical questions about the ownership and value of personal information. Should individuals have the right to own and profit from their data? How can fair compensation for the use of personal data be ensured? These questions are central to the ongoing discourse on data ownership and require a reevaluation of existing legal and economic frameworks.

Legal frameworks play a crucial role in protecting privacy and defining data ownership rights. The European Union's General Data Protection Regulation (GDPR), enacted in 2018, is a landmark regulation that seeks to address these issues. The GDPR grants individuals robust rights over their personal data, including the right to access, rectify, and erase data, as well as the right to data portability. It also imposes stringent requirements on organisations to obtain explicit consent, ensure data security, and provide transparency about data practices. By establishing clear guidelines and penalties for non-compliance, the GDPR aims to shift the balance of power towards individuals and enhance data protection.

Despite these regulatory efforts, the global nature of digital data flows presents significant challenges for enforcement and compliance. Data often crosses national borders, subject to varying legal standards and cultural norms regarding privacy. This transnational aspect necessitates international cooperation and harmonisation of regulations to ensure consistent protection of privacy and data ownership rights. Moreover, as technologies continue to evolve, regulatory frameworks must be adaptable and forward-looking to address emerging threats and challenges.

Technological solutions can also enhance privacy and data ownership. Privacy-enhancing technologies (PETs), such as encryption, anonymisation, and differential privacy, can protect personal data from unauthorised access and misuse. Encryption, for example, ensures that data remains confidential and secure, even if intercepted by malicious actors. Anonymisation techniques can remove identifying information from datasets, enabling data analysis without compromising individual privacy. Differential privacy adds noise to data, allowing for statistical analysis while protecting individual data points. By integrating PETs into data collection and processing practices, organisations can enhance data security and uphold ethical standards.

The concept of data stewardship offers another approach to addressing privacy and data ownership. Data stewardship involves organisations acting as responsible custodians of personal data, prioritising the interests and rights of individuals. This approach emphasises transparency, accountability, and ethical data practices, ensuring that data is used in ways that benefit individuals and society. Data stewardship can foster trust between individuals and organisations, enhancing cooperation and innovation while safeguarding privacy.

Public awareness and education are critical for empowering individuals to take control of their privacy and data ownership. Digital literacy initiatives can inform individuals about their rights and the implications of their data practices, enabling them to make informed decisions. Public awareness campaigns can highlight the importance of privacy and data protection, fostering a culture of accountability and responsibility. By raising awareness and promoting digital literacy, society can collectively advocate for stronger privacy protections and more equitable data ownership models.

The ethical and practical challenges of privacy and data ownership are significant and multifaceted. Navigating these challenges requires a comprehensive approach involving legal, technological, and educational strategies. Regulatory frameworks like the GDPR, privacy-enhancing technologies, data stewardship practices, and public awareness initiatives all play essential roles in protecting privacy and ensuring fair data ownership. By addressing these issues thoughtfully and collaboratively, society can harness the benefits of digital technology while safeguarding individual rights and autonomy. The discourse on privacy and data ownership will continue to evolve, but the commitment to ethical principles and protecting personal information must remain steadfast.

Social Media and the Future of Democracy

The advent of social media has fundamentally transformed the way democratic societies function. Platforms such as Facebook, Twitter, and Instagram have become central to political discourse, activism, and the dissemination of information. The ability of social media to connect people and amplify voices has been hailed as a boon for democracy, promoting engagement, transparency, and participation. However, the same characteristics that make social media a powerful tool for democratic engagement also present significant challenges, including the spread of misinformation, polarisation, and manipulation. Understanding the complex relationship between social media and democracy is crucial for navigating the future of democratic governance.

Social media platforms have undeniably revolutionised political communication. They provide politicians, activists, and ordinary citizens with direct channels to reach large audiences, bypassing traditional media gatekeepers. This democratisation of communication has enabled a more diverse range of voices to participate in public debates. Grassroots movements such as the Arab Spring, #BlackLivesMatter, and the global climate strikes have leveraged social media to organise, mobilise, and advocate for change. The ability to share information rapidly and widely has empowered individuals and communities to hold power to account and push for social justice.

Moreover, social media fosters transparency and accountability in democratic processes. Politicians and public officials use these platforms to communicate directly with constituents, share policy positions, and respond to public concerns. This direct engagement can enhance transparency and build trust between elected representatives and the public. Social media also serves as a watchdog, enabling citizens to expose corruption, misconduct, and abuses of power. Viral videos and hashtags have played a crucial role in bringing attention to issues that might otherwise have been overlooked by mainstream media.

Despite these positive aspects, the influence of social media on democracy is fraught with challenges. One of the most pressing concerns is the spread of misinformation and disinformation. Social media platforms, driven by algorithms that prioritise engagement, often amplify sensationalist and misleading content. This can distort public understanding of important issues and erode trust in democratic institutions. The COVID-19 pandemic, for instance, saw a deluge of false information about the virus and vaccines, undermining public health efforts and sowing confusion.

The phenomenon of echo chambers and filter bubbles further complicates the democratic landscape. Social media algorithms tend to show users content that aligns with their existing beliefs and preferences, creating insular communities where dissenting viewpoints are rarely encountered. This can reinforce ideological divisions and polarise public opinion, making constructive dialogue and compromise more difficult. The fragmentation of public discourse into isolated echo chambers undermines the deliberative aspect of democracy, where diverse perspectives are considered, and consensus is sought.

Manipulation of social media by malicious actors presents another significant threat to democracy. Foreign interference in elections, exemplified by Russia's meddling in the 2016 US presidential election, demonstrates how social media can be exploited to influence political outcomes. Coordinated disinformation campaigns, fake accounts, and bots can distort public perception and manipulate electoral processes. The ability of these actors to operate anonymously and at scale challenges the integrity of democratic systems and calls for robust measures to safeguard against such threats.

The role of social media companies in regulating content and ensuring the integrity of democratic processes is a contentious issue. These platforms wield enormous power in shaping public discourse and have been criticised for their lack of transparency and accountability. Decisions about what content to promote, demote, or remove are often made behind closed doors, with significant implications for free speech and democratic participation. The challenge lies in balancing the need to curb harmful content with the protection of free expression. Developing clear, consistent, and fair content moderation policies is essential for maintaining trust and legitimacy.

The ethical implications of data privacy and social media surveillance also relate to democracy. Social media companies' extensive data collection practices raise concerns about user privacy and the potential for surveillance. The Cambridge Analytica scandal revealed how personal data harvested from social media could be used to influence political behaviour, highlighting the need for stringent data protection measures. Ensuring that users have control over their personal information and that data is used ethically is crucial for safeguarding democratic values.

Addressing the challenges posed by social media requires a multifaceted approach involving governments, social media companies, civil society, and users themselves. Regulatory frameworks must be developed to ensure transparency, accountability, and the protection of democratic processes. Social media companies need to adopt ethical practices in content moderation, data privacy, and algorithm design. Civil society organisations play a vital role in advocating for user rights and promoting digital literacy. Educating the public about the ethical use of social media, critical thinking, and media literacy is essential for fostering a more informed and resilient democratic society.

The future of democracy in the age of social media hinges on our ability to navigate these complexities thoughtfully and ethically. By harnessing the positive potential of social media while addressing its challenges, we can strengthen democratic participation, enhance transparency, and protect the integrity of democratic processes. This endeavour requires ongoing dialogue, collaboration, and a commitment to democratic values. As social media continues to evolve, so too must our approaches to ensuring that it serves as a force for good in democratic societies.

Autonomy in the Digital Age

"Technology should enhance our autonomy, not erode it." – Shoshana Zuboff

Digital technology has transformed nearly every aspect of human life, offering unprecedented opportunities for convenience, connectivity, and efficiency. Yet, amidst these advancements lies a complex and often overlooked issue: the impact of digital technology on individual autonomy. Autonomy, the capacity to make informed, uncoerced decisions about one's life, is a cornerstone of personal freedom and self-determination. As digital technologies become more integrated into our daily lives, it is crucial to examine how they influence, enhance, or undermine this fundamental aspect of human existence.

Digital technologies, from smartphones and social media to artificial intelligence and the Internet of Things (IoT), have redefined the ways we interact with the world. These tools offer immense potential to empower individuals, providing access to information, facilitating communication, and streamlining everyday tasks. For example, AI-powered personal assistants like Siri and Alexa can help manage schedules, answer questions, and control smart home devices, offering a level of convenience previously unimaginable. Social media platforms allow users to express themselves, connect with others, and access a diverse array of perspectives, thereby enhancing personal and social autonomy.

However, these benefits come with significant challenges. One of the primary concerns is the extent to which digital technologies can infringe upon individual autonomy through surveillance and data collection. Every interaction online, whether it is a search query, a social media post, or a purchase, generates data that is often collected, analysed, and used by corporations and governments. This data can be used to track behaviour, predict preferences, and even manipulate decisions. The pervasive nature of digital surveillance raises important ethical questions about privacy, consent, and the control individuals have over their personal information.

The algorithms that power digital technologies also play a crucial role in shaping autonomy. These algorithms, designed to maximise engagement and efficiency, often operate invisibly, making decisions on behalf of users based on their data. For instance, recommendation systems on platforms like YouTube, Netflix, and Spotify suggest content that aligns with users' past behaviour, potentially limiting exposure to new and diverse information. While these recommendations can enhance user experience, they can also create echo chambers that reinforce existing beliefs and preferences, subtly influencing and restricting the autonomy of individuals.

Furthermore, the design of digital platforms can affect decision-making processes. Many digital interfaces are designed to be intuitive and user-friendly, but they can also be manipulative, employing techniques such as dark patterns to nudge users towards certain actions. Dark patterns are design elements that exploit cognitive biases to influence user behaviour, often leading to decisions that benefit the platform at the expense of the user's autonomy. Examples include making it difficult to opt-out of subscriptions, burying privacy settings, or using ambiguous language to obtain consent.

The rise of AI and machine learning introduces additional complexities. Autonomous systems, capable of making decisions with minimal human intervention, raise questions about accountability and control. For instance, autonomous vehicles, medical diagnosis systems, and financial trading algorithms operate with a degree of independence that can challenge traditional notions of human oversight and responsibility. Ensuring that these systems are transparent, explainable, and aligned with human values is essential to preserving autonomy in the digital age.

The concept of autonomy is also closely linked to digital literacy. As digital technologies become more pervasive, the ability to understand, navigate, and critically assess these technologies becomes crucial. Digital literacy empowers individuals to make informed decisions about their digital interactions, recognise potential biases, and safeguard their privacy. Promoting digital literacy through education and public awareness is fundamental to enhancing autonomy in the digital age.

Moreover, the ethical design of technology is vital to supporting autonomy. Designers and developers have a responsibility to create technologies that respect and enhance user autonomy. This involves prioritising user consent, transparency, and control, and avoiding manipulative practices that undermine these principles. Ethical design also means considering the broader societal impacts of technology and striving to create inclusive and equitable digital environments.

As we navigate the digital age, it is imperative to reflect on the ways technology shapes our autonomy and to seek a balance that maximises benefits while mitigating risks. The interplay between digital technology and autonomy is complex and multifaceted, requiring a concerted effort from individuals, technologists, policymakers, and society at large. By recognising and addressing the challenges posed by digital technologies, we can work towards a future where technology serves as a tool for empowerment and self-determination, rather than a source of control and constraint.

This chapter explores these themes in depth, examining the ways digital technologies impact autonomy and discussing strategies to protect and enhance individual autonomy in an increasingly digital world. Through this exploration, we aim to foster a nuanced understanding of autonomy in the digital age and to advocate for ethical practices that uphold this essential aspect of human dignity and freedom.

Freedom in the Digital Age

Autonomy is a fundamental concept in both philosophical and ethical discourse, representing the capacity of individuals to make informed, uncoerced decisions about their own lives. It is the bedrock of personal freedom, self-determination, and human dignity. In the digital age context, autonomy gains renewed importance and complexity as technological advancements increasingly shape our environment and decision-making processes.

At its core, autonomy is about self-governance. It encompasses the ability to reflect on one's desires, beliefs, and values and act according to these reflections. This involves acting according to one's immediate impulses and making choices that align with one's long-term goals and principles. Immanuel Kant famously associated autonomy with rationality, suggesting that to be autonomous is to act according to reason rather than mere inclination.

In practical terms, autonomy manifests in various aspects of life, from the personal to the political. Personal autonomy involves the freedom to make choices about one's body, lifestyle, and relationships without external interference. Political autonomy, on the other hand, relates to the capacity of individuals to participate in the governance of their communities, exercising their rights and responsibilities as citizens. Both dimensions of autonomy are essential for a flourishing society.

The digital age, characterised by the ubiquity of information technology and data-driven systems, poses significant challenges and opportunities for autonomy. Digital technologies have the potential to enhance autonomy by providing individuals with greater access to information, tools for self-expression, and platforms for civic engagement. For instance, the internet allows people to learn about diverse perspectives, pursue online education, and connect with like-minded communities. Social media platforms enable users to voice their opinions, organise collective action, and hold authorities accountable.

However, these same technologies can also undermine autonomy in subtle and pervasive ways. One of the primary concerns is the impact of digital surveillance and data collection. Every online interaction generates data that can be tracked, analysed, and used to influence behaviour. Companies and governments collect vast amounts of personal information, often without explicit consent, raising significant ethical questions about privacy and control. When algorithms predict and shape our choices based on this data, our capacity for genuine self-determination is compromised.

The design of digital technologies also plays a crucial role in shaping autonomy. Many platforms employ persuasive design techniques to capture and hold users' attention, often prioritising engagement over user well-being. Features such as endless scrolling, notifications, and personalised recommendations can create habits and dependencies that are difficult to break. These design choices can subtly manipulate behaviour, steering users towards certain actions and limiting their ability to make independent decisions.

Artificial intelligence (AI) further complicates the landscape of autonomy. AI systems, from recommendation engines to autonomous vehicles, make decisions that affect individuals' lives in profound ways. While these systems can enhance efficiency and convenience, they also raise questions about accountability and control. If an AI system makes a decision that impacts an individual's life, who is responsible for that decision? How can individuals ensure that these systems reflect their values and preferences? Ensuring that AI systems are transparent, explainable, and aligned with human values is essential for preserving autonomy.

Moreover, the rapid pace of technological change can itself be a barrier to autonomy. Keeping up with the latest developments, understanding their implications, and making informed choices about their use requires a high level of digital literacy. Many individuals lack the knowledge and skills to navigate this complex landscape effectively, leaving them vulnerable to exploitation and manipulation. Promoting digital literacy is therefore crucial for empowering individuals to exercise their autonomy in the digital age.

Ethical design and regulation are key to addressing these challenges. Designers and developers are responsible for creating technologies that respect and enhance user autonomy. This involves prioritising user consent, transparency, and control, and avoiding manipulative practices that undermine these principles. Regulators, meanwhile, must ensure that legal frameworks protect individuals' rights and hold organisations accountable for their data practices.

Ultimately, in the age of digitalization, human autonomy is still a pivotal point. The power of technology is double-edged as it, on the one hand, supports autonomy and, on the other hand, erodes it. Our decisions as a society will enable the balance to be achieved. By creating an environment in which the principle of self-determination is valued we can have the cake and eat it by enjoying the benefits of digital technology as well as maintaining the unalienable rights, which are the pillars of human dignity. The sustained debate about personal independence in the digital age is not so much about technology but even more about the type of society we want to build and the values we want to maintain.

Digital Autonomy and Human Agency

The recent onset of the digital revolution has reshaped our lives, jobs, and human dealings completely. At the epicenter of this transformation is the dynamic between digital autonomy and human agency. The former means individuals being in charge of their digital spaces and their personal details. The latter, on the other hand, refers to the individuals' ability to make decisions and act in line with the things that matter to them. The conflation of these two aspects is key in distinguishing the social ethical issues concerning new technologies and in ensuring that the digital upgrades fueling our progress enhance our self-determination but not restrain it.

The exponential development of digital tools like smartphones and computers, together with platforms such as social media and cloud services, are ideal communication, knowledge access and artistic tools for freedom of expression. They not only help one communicate easily with others but also they give them space to share ideas and foster self-expression. In particular, the internet has given everyone a reliable source of data and provided access to information in ways as never seen before.

Regardless of the many advantages, the pro-emancipative perspective has to confront a wave of powerful challenges. Critics argue that questions related to digital technologies' tendency to obstruct personal autonomy raise widespread anxiety. The biggest fear is the extent to which digital technologies could become a part of our personal lives. Digital activities, be it searching the web or engaging in social networks, are being tracked by these firms and governments to get the data they seek. This data is employed to track action, produce comprehensive profiles of clients, and manipulate choices. With these kinds of cyberattacks prepared to be launched, it is evident that people must be in control of the digital world and they must have autonomy over the data about their individual lives.

In addition, the technology that underlies data-driven models and dictate digital human behaviour and capabilities is of great importance. The following algorithms, designed to maximize interaction and harness human efficiency of experience, in some cases, act as substitutes for users and take decision based on users' data. The use of social media, for instance, shows content suggestions that reflect the behaviour of users. On the one hand, personalized content enhances user-experience by providing helpful information, on the other hand, it increases the risk of creating machines that create echo chambers by limiting exposure to multiple opinions, the result of which is a subtle transfer of the decision-making power of the users to the system, which in turn constrains the freedom of the users.

What influences human behavior is the design of digital interfaces. One good example is how digital companies employ dark patterns to seize and preserve the attention of a user. Such characteristics as notifications and infinite scrolling, embedded to suit the needs of the user are put in place to keep them entertained for longer. This kind of gratification is good for the company's profitability but it equally has the potential to turn individuals into helpless addicts who cannot decide their own digital usability consciously and cognitively.

Also, another significant connection between machine intelligence and individual control is the problem arising from the current scenarios of the human agency in digital space. However, that does not negate the fact that AI-powered intelligent systems are getting adopted in the day-to-day life of persons. AI systems, from chatbots to autonomous vehicles, should have already been making tough decisions for many individuals. Such systems function to an extent that offsets the traditional norms while users have total control in the digital realm. Where autonomous vehicles fitted with AI make every decision-related to driving when articulated by the machine and without any human interference. The most critical aspect of human agency preservation in a digitalized world is to allow AI systems to fully align with ethical and human values while still providing them with a set of rules that they have to follow.

Digital literacy is considered as another factor in digital self-determination and human empowerment. As the digital world we inhabit is establishing itself further, the ability to interpret, navigate, and evaluate critically these technologies is becoming all the more imperative. In that sense, being digitally literate means you are capable of making informed decisions about how and when to interconnect digitally, of detecting possible biases, and of protecting your privacy. Digital literacy is interwoven with educational programs and public awareness campaigns, as education has a significant impact on autonomy within a digital society for the citizens.

Another crucial ethical concern and effective means of solving these problems are ethics in design and regulation. Ethical practice in technology design and development presupposes ethics, such as respect for people, and promotes user autonomy, as designers and developers have the responsibility to create technologies, which respect individuals' rights and enable them to grow as autonomous beings. Key to this is to keep privacy configurations user-friendly and deny any manipulative actions. Certain examples include giving clear and accessible consent regarding data privacy, avoiding dark patterns, as well as ensuring that users have choice over the data that they keep or share.

Furthermore, regulation should be created to protect digital autonomy and human agency as well. The creation of frameworks that regulate digital autonomy also needs to be encouraged and empowered to protect the expectation of digital autonomy. The General Data Protection Regulation (GDPR) in the European Union is one example of a regulation that has been instrumental in setting precedents. These are regulations that protect individual rights concerning their digital data and impose duties upon data processors. Such regulations serve the purpose of allowing individuals full control over their digital habitat where their autonomy must be recognized. However, if the laws are not abided by, the regulations might lose their effectiveness over time, which might give rise to new issues related to their violation. Eventually, the regulations should be updated, when necessary, so that they are capable of coping with more advanced technological challenges and be able to guarantee that digital technologies are being utilized in a moral way.

For digital autonomy and human agency to have a fair future, it is important to have as many people from all corners as possible (i.e. technologists, politicians, NGOs, the ordinary people, etc.), participating in the debates that revolve around the ethics of digital technologies as well as actually doing the work of questioning and addressing possible problematic areas. Standing up for digital rights and the necessary ethical use of technologies can cause significant changes that provide the benefit of digital advancements to people in the society.

The connection between digital autonomy and human agency is quite intricate and variegated. Although the opportunities for autonomy are numerous in digital technologies, you must also keep in mind the challenges they pose in the process towards autonomy. Having in place an ecosystem that allows the recognition and delivery of individualism, we can not only deal with the aspects which are already running but also save the basic freedom that has formed the foundation for the dignity of every human. To make this successful, the deliberate space for conversation, cooperation, and adherence to ethical values is needed. We must change the way we approach ensuring the beneficial effects of digital technologies as they expand, which means that we ought to move away from the thought that they are the elements that help, not harm our autonomy and agency.

The Power and Responsibility of Algorithms

One of the barely noticeable essentials of the contemporary digital world are algorithms. Their one-of-a-kind properties serve as the groundwork for search engine functions, social media platforms, recommendations, and plenty of other apps, thus, leaving a vacuum in everyone's life. Even given the prevalence of these digital wonders, still, in many cases, the user could be deprived of a clear understanding of their functions or their whereabouts. The usage of algorithms in modern technology requires a systematic arrangement of instructions designed at the completion of a specific task or the resolution of a certain problem. In the digital context, algorithms interpret enormous datasets and make the best choices, offer advice, and improve the workflow. To put it in practice, the search engine algorithms input search words to fetch relevant outcomes, while on the social network, algorithms spot interesting users, and accordingly, the user's behavior, and preferences.

Maintaining and interpreting the large volumes of digital data produced in the modern age is one of the major tasks of algorithms. That enormous amount of data commonly branded as "big data" consists of information from searches and social media contacts like likes, or from past shopping episodes and location information on Google maps. Patterns, trends, and pairwise relevance owned by the data are usually computed with an algorithm facilitating it to be turned into strategic business smartness. It is due to the role of those pieces of advice that a wide spectrum of obligations ranging from securing patient operations to turning profit through marketing can be effectively fulfilled.

To the naked human eye, the figure multipliers of algorithms' users and interpreters in the era of digital technology can become so overpowering that they can become a real-time culture shock. Such pieces of such pieces of data refer to various activities, such as search queries and social media interactions, shopping histories, and location recordings. Algorithms are able to point out any semblance of systematics and trends as well as to track directly the volumes, which are of relevant importance regardless of the sector. With them, the fields of health and well-being have the following applications as a database assistant: Patient diagnosis-using them, doctors verify electronic health records and genomic data to predict medical vulnerabilities, approve offers of tailored medical treatment, and foresee disease outbreaks. Likewise, algorithms in the financial sector detect fraudulent transactions, assess the creditworthiness of the people involved, and then allocate investment funds. In the marketing business, algorithms customize advertising, predict consumer behavior, and segment the marketing base even further. These instances underline the enormous predictive power of algorithms to boost productivity, errorlessness and inventiveness.

However, the expanded adoption of algorithms is fraught with ethical and social concerns too. The primary one is an automatic bias. Acting only on the data they were trained on, the algorithms might support and even more lead to the biases. For instance, it was demonstrated that recognition algorithms might be more incorrect when people of color are them, so the bias from the training data is reflected. Fair datasets should be used in the same way because the algorithms are required for processes like legal enforcement, hiring and lending and if for example, the system is built using unfair data, it can be unfair to certain groups.

Therefore, the emergence of data bias through algorithms further complicates these issues. Many algorithms, especially those based on machine learning, operate as "black boxes" where the decision-making process is not transparent or easily understood. Lack of transparency introduces a greater challenge in spotting and remedying biases, holding systems accountable, and achieving fairness. While the computational process of developing algorithms that are not only accurate and efficient but also transparent and accountable is difficult.

Additionally, the unethical use of algorithms raises another sovereignty concern. It is a fact that algorithms often work with big data that collects information, but many fear how this data is accessed and protected. The scandal with Cambridge Analytica, using personal data from a large number of Facebook users without their knowledge, brought attention to the potential for data-driven algorithms to be misused. Making sure data is collected and handled in the right way with the appropriate consent and security mechanisms is immensely important to keep individual privacy inviolable and to ensure that public trust is maintained.

One of the critical points of discussion is the influence of algorithms on the public's opinions and judgment. Social media platforms' algorithms, driven by the desire to increase user engagement, tend to prioritize sensational and polarized content. This type of content fosters echo chambers where you mainly find information that reinforces your beliefs. This, in turn, leads to the deepening of the polarization in the society, as well as the establishment of propaganda. At the same time algorithms can be used as weapons in the hands of malicious actors to shape and influence political events. One important implication of this is that ethical guidance and control are needed.

Technological, political, and social dimensions are among the challenge areas. Technologists mustn't neglect the design and launching of algorithms in terms of ethical implications. In fact, this encompasses the development of ways to detect and remove biases, to ensure transparency and explainability, and to undertake privacy protection comprehensively with confidence. Ethical design practices need to be interwoven into the algorithms' entire life cycle- right from conception to deployment through maintenance

Another significant role is that of policymakers in creating regulatory laws and mechanisms that ensure the ethical use of algorithms. Although these regulations would be based on some of the following principles of equity, accountability, and transparency, the government should introduce regulation for the impact of algorithms, independent audits, and a situation where people are compensated if they are harmed. Besides, it should not be forgotten that digital technologies and data flows are global in nature, something that calls for concerted efforts to bring cooperation among different countries.

There is no denying that the combination of public knowledge and education is the greatest factor driving a more informed and participatory society. By becoming aware of how algorithms impact and shape our daily life, and developing skills that allow them to critically assess such algorithmic decisions, people can use literacy rights as initiatives to improve literacy rates on the Internet and understand them. With the help of digital literacy programs, people can become familiar with the mechanism behind the algorithms, notice possible biases and assert their own rights. Thus, by involving the public in the discussions about the ethical use of algorithms we strive to achieve general principles and values that everyone accepts.

To be precise, algorithms making their presence felt in the contemporary society are characterized as powerful but, at the same time, as a complex mechanism. While they speed up the flow of business, facilitate good performance, and innovation, they also climax into tough situations where people are challenged ethically and socially. Tackling these dual dimensions involves a multipronged approach where algorithms should be responsibly created and utilized. That is, through being open, being held accountable, and practically remaining impartial, we can finally appreciate the potential of algorithms as a means to advance humanity plu. this terms that our values and rights are no left behind.

The Future of Digital Autonomy

An informative content style that focuses on delivering checked facts.

The rapidly evolving technology taking place in these days makes the impulse of digital autonomy greatly noticed. As digital technology in human life becomes more complex, it becomes a necessity to strike a balance between individual development and the rights of individuals. The future of the digital age may lie in finding consensus between technical ingenuity, moral reflection, and law-based regulations for the sake of human agency in a digital society.

One of the remarkable achievements leading to the concept of digital autonomy is the rise of artificial intelligence (AI). There is an increasing number of AI applications integrated into daily life, including virtual assistants, personalized recommendations, self-piloting cars, and smart home devices. All of these innovations provide more choices when they are in use. They also boost one's convenience, efficiency, and personalization of experiences. On the other hand, these innovations represent new privacy challenges related to digital autonomy. These challenges, need to be checked by addressing such issues as data privacy and algorithmic decisions.

Given the ever-growing human surveillance and data collection, it is also a gradual process in the development of AI technologies. As mentioned, these technologies collect data from numerous sources and analyze browsing histories to create personalized experiences. The company defends its position on data sharing by showing that customers are offered services that exceed their expectations because the company uses their personal data. However, the designing of AI systems to be more private entails huge amounts of data. Furthermore, the individuals' unawareness of privacy issues can lead to the misuse of data. The protection of the individual and the company's rights should be the ethical issue for development companies.

There is a rise in blockchain technology which holds a bright future for digital liberty. The common ledger known as blockchain makes sure of safe and transparent transactions without involving any intermediaries. This technology in use could provide people with new freedom because it locate the power to the individual's digital identity and the usage of data. To illustrate, decentralised identity systems enable individuals to control their own credentials and decide with whom to share their personal data and do not rely on trusted intermediaries. Blockchain through decentralizing data storage, security, and ownership can assure better protection from data breaches and information misuse.

Pivotal to the concept of digital autonomy is the improvement of privacy-enhancing technologies (PETs) that give a good opportunity to share without neglecting crowd privacy. These tools, such as differential privacy, homomorphic encryption, and secure multi-party computation allow for data manipulation without a compromise with individual data privacy. Men while girls love to see what they have to say about a different paradise let me see the phone numbers. Differential privacy, for example, adds noise to data sets so that it is impossible to identify a particular individual, so one can still undergo some useful data analysis while retaining his privacy. Moreover, homomorphic encryption allows computations to be carried on the encrypted data, thus guaranteeing that no one knows what kind of data is included in the process. This combined with the addition of privacy-enhancing technology in digital technology can bring together the benefits of data-driven innovation with the protection of privacy.

An added significant factor that determines the future of digital autonomy is the concept of digital sovereignty. Digital sovereignty is the right of a person, or a country decides his/her personal or national digital space. With the prevailing issues of data localization and national security, countries are now looking for ways to take control of their digital space. This creates in turn a need for policies that will look at the efficient and compliant flow of data across borders, international cooperation, and the digital world economy globally. It is crucial to not sacrifice the principles of openness and cooperation in order to promote a common digital landscape of fairness and justice that will be the result of achieving the balance between digital sovereignty and the principles of openness and collaboration.

Regulatory policies will continue to play a critical role in shaping digital freedom. A good example is Europe's GDPR, which has set some standards for data protection and personal rights. The legislation to come will have to treat various issues: ethical applications of AI, the fairness of digital identities, and the decentralization of technologies. The way to that is the international collaboration for creating standards and providing digital autonomy across borders.

The ethical design of digital technologies is another cornerstone of that future digital world. Presence of a good user experience should be put first by designers and developers, as well as their roles to assure that users are informed, treated justly, and given free will in systems operation. Part of the responsibility is to ensure that the ideas the digital systems are based upon are freer, inclusive, and humane.

Digital literacy seems to be a more significant puzzle piece in helping people to cope with the digital world phenomenon. It is fundamental to understand that technology and skills will always evolve simultaneously. Teaching programs which emphasize digital literacy, critical thinking, and an understanding of digital rights serve as a basis to instruct individuals for them to make reasoned choices about their digital media interactions. Thus, through digital literacy, the sense of personal autonomy, resiliency against technological changes may flourish in a society.

The future of digital autonomy isn't only about technology or regulation. But it also has a significant role to play in the field of public engagement and advocacy and this will have a pivotal effect. Engaging people from different social, economic, and professional backgrounds and creating constructive dialogues about the ethical and social implications of digital technologies are some of the high potential methods to identify some of the possible problems and create a common inclusive solution. Serving as an advocate of digital rights, privacy, and ethical technology will lead to a more positive change and ensure that the profits of digital innovation are shared justly.

The future looks like an era where the border drawn between technological innovativeness, ethical interest and legal requirements will essentially point to the outcomes of preserving the digital autonomy. Apart from cyber safety rules, decentralization, and ethical design, privacy improves can be used that breakthrough technology that will provide privacy and respect the people's individual liberty. The continuous conversation about digital autonomy should be a guide in the digitalization process through the problems of the digital age, that the digital tools are only a servant rather than a master.

The Digital Divide: Access and Equity

"The internet is not a luxury, it is a necessity." – President Barack Obama

Digital technologies and the internet have reformed the digital era* of ours making the internet and digital technologies inevitable parts of everyday life. They have brought about revolutions in various sectors such as the work, education, health, and socialisation. Virtual reality has become the new reality where we find our young generation playing games on-line, e-learning through blackboards and smartboards. Digital divide looms as a significant issue in society, and disparities in digital access serve to highlight the crucial problem of equity as those being left without access to digital resources are getting further and further marginalized at a time when all day long the world is putting more emphasis on being digitalized.

The digital divide incorporates several aspects, for instance, accessibility of hardware and internet services, the ability to read, write, comprehend and communicate via the digital platform, and employs digital electronics, among others. At the most fundamental level, this divide is evidenced by the great disparity present between those who are connected to the internet and are equipped with digital devices and those who are not connected. This access is influenced by various factors including socioeconomic status, geographic location, age, and educational background. For instance, rural and remote areas mainly face the problem of lack of infrastructure, with limited or no internet access being an ordinary occurrence there. Similarly, people from lower socioeconomic status may not be able to afford the required digital devices and internet service.

The digital gap cannot be taken as a minor problem as it tends to have an impact in various life areas. In education, students who do not have access to digital technologies are at the brink of getting extinct in an increasingly "Hi-Tech" education environment. They cannot use online resources, cannot join online classes, and they cannot also utilize distance education digital tools. This was vividly seen during the COVID-19 pandemic, where schools across the globe switched to online learning. Those students who didn't have the proper digital access were left behind by being subject to cumulative educational inequalities. These kids who have no digital access may have long-term impacts, which can limit not only the academic achievements of the students but also their life opportunities.

**Note: It would be more reader-friendly if we used 'era' in the original text by introducing it as "The" at the beginning of the sentence since the topic has not been previously mentioned, so we can avoid circle wordiness and we can use one us "the" for. Then we rephrased "The internet and digital technologies have made the digital era a reality…" depending on the subject, and it made some more logical sequences. **

The use of the digital has become incredibly essential, especially in relation to employment. We know that many job applications, most future interviews, and any necessary training are routinely conducted online. This calls for a significant amount of reliable internet access and digital skills. Workers in areas lagging behind in digital use or those who are digitally challenged encounter huge stumbling blockages to jobs and careers. Furthermore, the trend of remote work and gig economy will continue to grab many jobs that digital access has been proven as a big factor in the process of economic participation. People who are not connected digitally are separated from what they could take part in to a full extent.

Healthcare is also where the digital divide causes stigma. The digital health technologies including telemedicine and another telehealth service present great potential for enhancing care access, particularly in underprivileged areas. But, still, the point is one and only digital access. Someone without a computer and a smartphone does not qualify for a virtual consultation, and that leads to health disparities. Not only is medical patients' digital health literacy a foundational skill needed for accessing online health resources but also for these individuals to manage their own electronic health records and partake in the digital health projects.

The digital divide impacts social relations and civic engagement as well. Social media platforms are often the sites where people come together, become part of communities, and communicate through the internet. And, the people who don't have a digital way can not even be part of all these members in the first place. As a result, they can not get involved in any communal events, obtain information, or take part in public debate. Consequently, the digital divide impacts political involvement by serving as places for major political interactions, protests, and referendums. By not acquiring digital access individuals will be left unsupported to be full participants of the democracy run.

As for making a puncture in the digital gap, one must use a number of approaches such as infrastructure development, digital literacy, and inclusive design. The pivot in evading digital divide is laying the foundation of a technical infrastructure. This means spreading the network and ensuring that modern technologies access the high-speed internet in areas that are remote and rural in particular. To help achieve such an aim, policymakers should think of state and federal support for public and private sector organizations involved in the initiative. They would provide the resources, help set up and expand the digital infrastructure for instance. Furthermore, rules and activities that focus on lowering the cost of internet and digital devices can also lift up affordability, thus making internet usage more easy to handle for people of low incomes.

Digital literacy is the other pivotal piece in achieving the digital divide. Equipping individuals with the skills and information necessary for using digital technologies is essential for the actual involvement of people in digital processes. The use of digital environments and communication channels for learning and for practical solutions can be fostered through school programs, seminars, and associations that concentrate on digital literacy skills. It includes the teaching of basic computer operation, internet surfing, online safety, as well as participation in digital and print communication used in teaching, communicating, and for job search.

Technology has to be developed with the specific use of design principles to build digital technologies and platforms that are accessible to all individuals, and that can indeed be used by them equally regardless of the unique abilities that they possess, or the unique conditions where they live. This includes making interfaces that are easy to learn and easy to use, providing disability access, and taking into account the specific needs of users. The developers of technology, by promoting how inclusive their platform is can manage to involve very many people in using their programs such that they become visible in the digital world favoring equity.

The consideration of public policy and advocacy is very important as the best possible means of handling the challenge of the digital divide and expediting digital equity. Digital justice is of the highest importance to policymakers, who have to accept the challenge of inclusion in their agendas and appreciate how digital access supports social and economic engagement. This spells a need for programs where all the infrastructure, affordability, literacy, and inclusivity issues will be addressed. In Poor Communities, Lobbying Activities Can Raise General Awareness Tying it to Digital Equality and Galvanizing Support for All Actions Designed to Overcome the Divide.

International cooperation is also essential in addressing the global dimensions of the digital divide. The slightest access to digital means is not only the problem of individual countries but a global issue that gravely impacts the countries on different degrees, depending on the development scale. Efforts like joint projects, conferences, and tech exposition for example between countries, international organizations, and the world's leading information technology companies would promote the dissemination of information and resources, while the best practices prevalent would be followed in a general way to resolve the issues of inferiority in the digital sphere. Large-scale international projects that aim to develop digital infrastructure, instil digital literacy and guarantee affordable access will contribute to overcoming the digital divide on a global scale.

The private sector has a significant role to play in bridging the digital divide. Additionally, tech companies will need to come in with cheaper technologies, connectivity to digital infrastructure, and digital literacy programs which will make them part of the solution. Digital inclusion among other corporate social responsibility projects that are anchored in the public sector and tailored to local communities leaves a lasting effect. Private sector companies should be involved and their experience and resources should be utilized to overcome digital disparity.

Our ability to face the digital divide in its complexity, and with inclusion in mind, is the central problem that will decide the future of digital parity - will we be able to conquer it? Peacock, 6); it is not just social justice, but also economic progress. Refolding For those who have a cracked code, it is not of equity alone but also of social and economic progress. We cannot lose sight of the main goal, which is "powering digital connectivity" - In this way, we will be able to unleash technology on an unprecedented scale and create an environment where both innovation and creativity will thrive. As one of the consequences of facilitating work-openness and participatory innovation, digital technologies foster inclusion and empowerment for all members of the society. Our everyday life in digital space becomes more open for everybody to access. From whatever factor, it is a work in progress if we want to defy these issues and secure a brighter digital future for everyone.

Understanding the Digital Divide

Expressed in broad terms, the digital divide is indeed a multifaceted and dynamic problem often related to unequal access to underpinning technologies. Recapping the problems encountered by people needing technology one should say that it is a technical problem, at the same time it involves the dimensions of a society – being it socio-economic, geographical, and cultural ones finally influencing the digital age. Amongst the diverse fields of technology, education, the labor market, health, and social life the understanding of the digital divide is vital for a balanced approach to the development of the social order and opportunities for everyone are equal.

At the root, the digital divide is visible through the three forms of access, the quality of that access, and the skills to effectively use digital tools. Conversely, internet access and availability of digital devices expose the first and most noticeable feature. In localities dealing with the problems of rurality and distantness, individuals often suffer from lack of basic connectivity. The poverty of internet penetration, in those areas, is obtainable due to a material thinking pattern with the cause stated as the economic harshness, distant places, and because of poor telecommunication infrastructure. Also, abundant in urban and semi-urban areas where there is adequate infrastructural development, low-income households may be unable to subscribe to superfast broadband or buy up-to-date digital devices which widen the divide even more.

The second and quite critical aspect of the digital divide is related to the quality of the access. It is not only sufficient but also actually important to understand that merely having access to the internet does not mean anything if it is slow, both ends are unreliable, or, restricted. Additionally, infrastructure serves as the backbone for advanced digital application types such as video, teleconferencing, cloud services, and streaming and it affects everything from online learning to telehealth and digital entertainment. Multiple instances occur where the digital divide is a reality due to the poor connection that some regions have and their technological underdevelopment beside the urban and rich regions.

One of the essential but often overlooked components of the digital gap is digital literacy. Possessing digital gadgets and internet access does not necessarily mean that efficient usage will be produced. Digital literacy includes the set of skills as well as the knowledge required to recognize, evaluate, and create information with the help of digital technologies. It pertains to the most basic capabilities such as running a computer and internet exploration but also to a more-advanced set of skills such as programming, data analysis, as well as cybersecurity knowledge. In the absence of digital literacy, people are not able to participate in the digital economy and society to the fullest, no matter the adequacy of their access to technology is.

But the socioeconomic dimensions of the digital divide are closely tied to the issues of income, education, and social status. Low-income and less educated people are not so much in access and using digital technologies satisfactorily. As a result, this digital difference leads inevitably to the generation of poor people and people deprived of equal efficiency and thus, the social promoting power of technology. It is student-oriented environments from primary schools to universities that are fundamental in breaking bridges between different classes by offering educational strategies to students of underserved communities.

Geographical gaps do even more to the digital divide. Demographics find that urban areas in so many countries often have been blessed with commendable digital infrastructure and online services whereas things are completely the opposite for rural and isolated places. It is not only the dividing factor between the urban and rural areas in the nations but also a common problem in the region of the developed world and other countries. In these rural settings, digital literacy must be a common denominator for everyone if they want to have equal access to a very useful and cheap source of information and knowledge. This kind of remote region positions only makes sense if take into account other economic elements that lead to hardship in solving the digital divide.

The digital divide arises from the technological and cultural divergence. Most internet content is in English, which is as an example marginalizes non-English speakers, which, consequently, restricts them from having access to the information they need and then pursuing opportunities. Also, how communities perceive technology and education and set cultural attitudes has a direct impact on how much the people of these communities engage with digital tools. In the context of the digital divide, dealing with cultural and linguistic barriers implies creating digital content which is more harmonious and more diversified so that the content can encompass a larger audience.

The digital divide results from technological and cultural differences, which is crippling in several life aspects. For instance, in the field of education, the absence of reliable internet connections, and digital device ownership make it complicated for students to keep pace with their classmates in completing their school points or using their learning resources via the internet. During the global restrictions of movement, "online learning" is a learning method that requires students and teachers to go online for learning purposes. However, despite critical situations like the COVID-19 pandemic, students from digitally marginalized areas of education became further left behind, thus worsening the existing educational inequality.

In terms of job-related problems, the digital divide hampers the access to job positions and career promotion. Nowadays, different types of employment applications and discussions with each other to find people who can accompany you in your career path are both implemented online. Consequently, digital literacy and internet connectivity are fundamental prerequisites. Nowadays, the existence of remote work has become more common, especially when COVID-19 spread, and that is mostly dependent on reliable internet access and essential software skills. Workers located in geographically isolated areas or those without digital capabilities are the most vulnerable in the highly competitive job market of today.

Healthcare is also heavily affected by the digital divide. In particular, telehealth services are digital technologies that allow remote consultations and online medical advice, offering first-class access to healthcare anywhere in the world. However, there are many sub-contexts to this and one of them is the digital access that is basic for these services to work. People with no online facility or a digital device are not able to access telehealth services. For instance, residents in rural areas who do not have the privilege of good telehealth services are exposed to worsened healthcare services which can cause various problems in their health.

Another branch of the life influenced by this is the digital divide has to be the social participation and civic engagement. Social media platforms and other computer-mediated communication tools promote relations and involvement in society.

Equally, those people in the community who do not have electronic access are alienated from these social networks and, therefore, are hindered in community activities and information retrieval. Furthermore, digital platforms have been encouraging even more political participation that includes activism, discussion, and voting. The rational argument is that the prevalent digital divide may hamper people from practicing their rights in the democratic process.

Erasing the digital divide requires a holistic and multi-faceted strategy. It is a collaboration between governments, private sector entities, and civil society organizations to take depressing trends in various areas like digital access, connectivity improvement as well as digital literacy to eradicate the digital divide. Availability of high-speed internet, especially in rural and underprivileged areas, can only be possible by investing in the digital infrastructure. Programs and implementations intended to lessen internet costs for households can reduce the digital Penetration Divide. The digital accessibility entertainment problem is exacerbated by not only being cut off from accessing the software but also being deterred by the high prices of the type of gadget.

In giving priority to digital literacy, the inclusion of digital skills in the school and university curriculums is a critical way of enabling students to master digital tools that are crucial for their professional life and personal aspects. At school, we should introduce the concept of digital literacy and educate students on how to apply it since digital literacy plays a huge role in the development of a person's life.

Community organizations can provide digital skills courses and assistance to adults, particularly to those living in disadvantaged regions.

The private sector plays an important role in overcoming the digital divide by having information technology companies produce and make cheap digital solutions in the upcoming future, and they also should invest in the digital infrastructure. Companies also need to participate in the digital literacy and digital infrastructure development of different regions. To be specific, corporate social responsibility even the access to digital resources play major roles.

Describing and spotting the digital rift is absolutely necessary or in other words, we need to be sure that people are part of the digital wave. By defining it in a more comprehensive way and not just saying it, we can put in place policies that cater to a digital consortium where there is a fair distribution of information for everybody.

The Ethical Implications of Access

New technological advancements and the internet have come a long way and have impacted the whole world to a split into what the both sides are. This has consequently established systems that, on the one hand, facilitate the communication and movement of people, but on the other, have an equally unfortunate sickening effect where disadvantage also grows to even incontestable heights. Several objects, as well as delivery of services and their immediacy, account for the removal of distance between two parties in the first category of the advantages brought by the Internet and other digital technologies. However, the symptoms of these gifts are not always identical therefore, the issue of inequality could be equally displayed as a result of the access to the digital resources. It is in this sense that the dilemmas raised about the ethical use of technology and the quality of access prove public policy needs to be given. Thereby ethical considerations related to access, through which their absence or lack of digital training is noted, have involved topics of fairness, justice, personal privacy, and the responsibility of the different actors in the sectors to make sure that the technology advancement level is fit for everyone with more levels of exclusion.

Connectedness to digital technology and the web alike had started shuffling the priority list of essentials from smartly assigned other points of air or information to partly rights that should be fought for like, say, electricity and wireless water supply. Having everything such an essential relationships between that digital connection and gaining access that it is an indispensable key to use the e-government services, representing one's own community in the public sphere and also expanding knowledge and skills through interconnectedness. In contrast, a large number of people are excluded from this platform because of unobtaining skills of ICT(Finger, 2014). Broadband internet connections have become a popular mode of communicating and doing business due to its high data transfer rate and stability. However, there seems to be a divide that preference to the youth and wealthier customers. It is a truth, that the internet of things is among the most critical lifelines that can improve the welfare of people if easily accessible.

One of the most recurring doubts is whether it is ethical to treat this access as substantive as justice. There is a consensus among the experts that fairness in digital access means that everyone, irrespective of their financial standing, area of residence, age, or special needs, can enjoy the benefits that come from computer technologies. Thus making internet connectivity not an option but a reality, among all individuals as it also adds up to their guaranties of fundamental services which they so feel part of, or some communication is happening in their rights. In all fairness, it is often a matter of how resources are allocated which bear major liberals' dissatisfaction with digital systems depending on how much citizen voice is considered during the design and implementation of e-governance. A failure to manage this makes it impossible to strive for social justice because prevent inequitable distribution of goods.

One place where the ethical aspects of access have come to bear is in the educational environment. Even if online learning, utilization of a wide-connectivity database, and digital collaboration opportunities are examples that show the change in educational strategies thanks to digital technology, there are still students who do not have stable internet connections or digital devices and thus are disadvantaged which results in the lack of involvement in digital learning. This digital divide stymies the educational system and reduces the chances of lower-class individuals for academic progress and the future do not guarantee them that they would be on a better economical or career level in the future. In the world of Education, the issue of ensuring that all students get access to digital learning tools, is critical as it develops clarifications of educational inequities and the need to aid individuals to self-actualize.

Similarly, in healthcare, the ethical considerations relating to patient access through the digital service are also deep. One way in which the utilization of digital tools can improve healthcare is through telemedicine and digital health services. They become especially useful for patients who find themselves in remote and underserved areas which lack easy and systematic access to hospitals and doctors. This also speeds up obtaining of healthcare services since the requirement of distance and travel no longer exists, even though it will lead the decision-makers to have to face that challenge factors that ensure the provision of health services of which this aspect is one of them. Still, the health demand for digital health rests on the issue of inclusiveness. If someone does not have internet access or digital literacy, they cannot access those services which then leads to health inequality in terms of access and outcomes. The ethical treatment of all society members requires the elimination of the barriers that stand in their access to digital health services.

Privacy is another critical ethical considerations governing digital access. The collection, storage, and use of personal data by digital platform vendors present legitimate concerns related to digital justice. Even though the unrestricted digital participation of people in the digital environment and economy contributes to wider social inclusion it also makes those persons vulnerable to potential privacy risks. On the one hand, assuring the privacy of digital users makes the use of strong data protection and data regulation organized in a transparent way necessary. Users, on the other hand, should be given information as to how their data is collected and used and be asked for their consent before using it.

Different players, including nations, businesses as well as civic organizations, have on them the responsibility to make sure of equal opportunity in access, which is one of the strategic ethical issues. Governments have an exclusive role in attempting to work out appropriate policies promoting digital inclusion. Besides investments in digital infrastructure, special attention should be paid to the provision of internet services at a lower cost; this also includes computers and other necessary devices necessary for low-income families. The promotion of digital literacy like educating and training are the other ways through hosting these types of endeavors in education and training by which they could harmonize it into their offices.

The private sector companies, specifically website development ones, have another responsibility related to ethical access. One of the things they are capable of doing is developing affordable devices. They may also invest in extending digital infrastructure and assisting digital inclusion programs. Companies should also try to imbibe the culture of being responsible for social pursuits such as thu bridging of the digital gap most of which are performed together with the public sector. The advancement in technology is also indicated by the availability of privacy protection throughout and proper use of data protection practices.

Non-governmental organizations are also the important actors in the fight for the digital environment where fair rules are set and the opportunities are broadest. Activism and participation should be seen as major tools that these organizations use in their advocates for digital equity and getting involved in the act of promoting access. They can spread the knowledge about the separation in the field of modern technologies and also provide some preliminary training in digital skills. Another possible solution is organized, community-based efforts that people in communities take by themselves. By joining forces with the government as well as the businesses, non-profit organizations can contribute to designing and putting into action relevant strategies for the advancement of digital inclusion.

Accesses ethical dimensions go beyond the personal and societal sphere and extend to global concerns. The digital divide is a universal dilemma that has led to huge inequalities in IT matter and digital infrastructure between countries. This is why it is crucial to ensure Global Digital Equity: close cooperation across the world, sharing of resources, and exemplified best practices. In-kind payments and technical partnerships are among the methods that wealthy countries and international bodies can lend a hand to their poorer counterparts. The fairness of the digital world is reflected in its global character and accordingly, we should strive for global digital equity for all to thrive.

After ensuring global digital equality, we can still not ignore the fact that we need to prepare in advance to tackle the ethical issues that might arise. Along with the advent of new technologies like artificial intelligence and the Internet of Things, the ethical issue of assuring equal access to these technologies becomes even more critical. Now, that the digital infrastructure has jurisdiction over the world, it is essential to understand that the digital divide is not only a matter of connection but also the disadvantaged users' relationship to technology. And it is entirely up to digital literacy and law alongside the protection of ethical and inclusive principles that will be functional in this regard. Apart from predicting the possible effects of these technologies and tackling ethical concerns proactively, it must be in the first place to safeguard the right of access for all citizens by ensuring global digital equity.

The significance of ethics for the successful deployment of digital technologies in society is immense, as they outline the areas one must first address. By safeguarding digital rights of freedom through encryption, consent, and accountability mechanisms, we look at the world with optimism as technological opportunities are there for everyone to explore. It is, therefore, of paramount importance that we shall stick to our ethical tasks of protecting independence and dealing with the barriers that digital access brings about. This requires not only a genuine commitment to ethical practice but also to the elimination of the obstacles preventing access to the digital world.

Equity in Digital Education

Digital technology offers a lot of learning, collaboration, and access to information to those who otherwise wouldn't or couldn't afford it, which didn't exist in the past. There are numerous tools that fall under digital education, such as different apps, online courses, virtual classes, and so on. But the digital divide requires discussions about the distribution of resources among the various groups, missing the point of equality. It is vital that every student has equal opportunities and resources provided by digital learning which is the base of justice and inclusive educational systems.

Equality in the digital education system stands for the notion that no matter the students' social status, geography, or personal background, out of all digital learning tools and resources, they are at their disposal. The correction of these differences in internet kinks, computing device availability, and digital proficiency is mandatory. The lack of these elements stands like a wall to have fairness in education.

Thus, it brings us to the most significant issue with equity in digital education, which is unequal access to digital gadgets and internet services. Poorer students are highly unlikely to afford technological devices due to the unaffordable price, and this is the only part of their insufficient budget to be actually connected to the internet. This is a barrier to effective use the internet for learning and the access to digital educational resources. Schools and governments need to coordinate their efforts to ensure the engineering and operation of an infrastructure that allows everyone in need to use technology.

The digital divide is very much fuelled by geographical imbalances. The students in rural and remote areas usually bear the cross of lacking proper internet infrastructure that often has limited or unreliable connectivity. The essential result of this is decreasing their participatory functions in online and face-to-face learning and is a major factor harming getting the same educational opportunities as their fellow urban students. The only way to narrow the gap is to inject specific funds into the expansion of the broadband infrastructure that covers even remote areas.

Equity in digital education also depends on digital literacy. You should have your own digital gadgets with internet access for learning if you don't have the skills and knowledge of using them. Digital literacy is a wide array of knowledge - a person should have computer skills, the ability to navigate through the internet, and to be able to determine which online content is reliable or not. This often includes knowledge about online safety, digital content credibility, and basic computer skills. Not being familiar of such skills is a sign that there are strongly students or individuals that are unable to optimize all the information and resources in their use. As a primary mean of fostering digital literacy, schools ought to make its integration an important part of the curriculum and emanate teaching aids and content which are also useful in the safe and effective use of digital devices that the students will have.

During the COVID-19 pandemic digital equity in Education became central amidst the strong impacts of covid 19 on education worldwide. When schools worldwide went for remote learning, those students without a digital chance were left behind favoring the widening of the academic disparity that exists in the system. The pandemic brought to light the reality that the more comprehensive measures must be put in place to equip all student members with digital resources such as a strong digital infrastructure, affordable internet access, and thorough digital literacy programmes, among others. These issues have to work in parallel in schools which are the nerve and heart of building resilient and exclusive educational systems in case of a progressive digital era.

Teachers as well as educators are instrumental in making digital education a more equitable field. A well-versed department staff should be created, and teachers should also be trained on how to utilize digital tools in the educational process. This is important because teachers are among the crucial ones who need high-quality training to ensure that they can effectively use digital tools for teaching and learning purposes in classrooms and that they can efficiently inform the students on the issue of the digital world. They should also learn faculty and staff to be confident in using those digital resources both inside and outside school. interaction with the preachers also makes them interact freely with the students. Teachers, for example, can introduce new technologies into their classrooms as a way of imparting knowledge to the children. Every student has their own learning style and they use different levels of technology learning according to their needs, this is a deepening of cultural parameters, and therefore forms an essential part of it as every student can benefit. Along with the teachers' readiness, the availability of provision for the students to acquire the skills is equally important, i.e. the use of a wide range of technological equipment in the school for all educational programs. This also applies to the social dimension, in terms of the ability to develop networks within a community that will empower the members to work, think, and cooperate.

Beyond the aforementioned points, the universal, or say it is correct in each place, precepts of inclusivity are employed to achieve equality in digital education. Assistive technologies and digital education materials used in school cannot assist with the social aspect, though they are only helpful in the process of teaching and entertainment. Hence, the need for alternatives to devices persecuted by students had to be sought. For those students with needs, the modification of the content description into audio or video format, as well as the tools that facilitate different learning styles and approaches, is mandatory. By focusing on the hands of children who attend both regular and adaptation schools, training sessions can be held. It is then up for the parents to make the first move by enabling their children to carry out different exercises themselves, both independently and in co-operation with others. It's also a digression to say that the family's social behaviour is significant. You have found several points that need to be further investigated and you also gap few studies to go simply to show possible linkage or similarities. It also serves to mention what additional research will need to be done alongside this study on the subject.

In the advancement for digital education, not the teachers in the first place but mainly the parents and the community need to take part of the leadership. In a postmodern world, the teachers also have to update their skills and develop with the social and material changes to get the same respect and trust as they are. To begin with, the parents' obligation in staying close to their children in every aspect of learning is crucia. Especially for the parents with the long distance to go and see their children, they can use that chance just to keep track of the lessons and what they do at school through a webcam from anywhere. Equally participation in activities by community organizations and municipal authorities is vital to achieving these goals. The project will be rendered successful through making available the hardware, Internet services to the rural areas, digital training, and developing an enabling environment, these organizations can make significant contributions to have knowledge transferred.

Policy makers and leadership in the academic institutions must make it a priority to bridge this gap in the internet global system and digital literacy there. This caps the development of the courses in both the public and private sectors. Policy will be the main area of focus for education adminstrators, and different strategies ought to be developed to achieve digital equity. Policymakers, then, are the readers of the digital equity in their districts. Ensuring equity in digital education can be achieved by investing in digital infrastructure, granting subsidies for internet access and devices, and organizing professional development for educators, thus improving the digital education curriculum. Furthermore, the development of such policies must be evidence-based so as not to overlook certain challenges that diverse populations may face in their education systems.

Equally, international cooperation is key to digital equity. The digital divide is not limited to individual states but is the worldwide problem that creates a lot of digital inequality. The collaborative work between countries and international organizations and global technology companies could lead to enhancement, capacity-sharing, and up-to-date methods for eliminating digital inequities. In conclusion, ensuring access to digital resources around the world is a fundamental condition for inclusive and sustainable human development.

The future of education is going to be more and more digital, and it's very essential to have digital equity for the students to become future digital citizens. For example, by providing more and more technology/eBooks that are accessible for almost everyone. The first step toward putting everything into practice is leveling the access to it by removing the digital divide. That is, schools through their teachers should take the initiative by creating a learning environment that integrates all the students. For these reasons, all those in charge, teachers, commissioners, community-based organizations, and the private sector must work together to devise and execute digital equity programmes. With these tools of cooperation, all our students can grow beyond their expectations around their digital life.

Economic Impact of the Digital Divide

The problem of digital divide involves the unequal access to internet and digital technologies, which is a significant economic issue. There is a gap that keeps growing in the digital resources between those who have them and those who don't in today's world economy which digital infrastructure and connectivity have become the main drivers of, posing significant socio-economic inequalities. The uneven distribution of digital resources worsens the gap between rich and poor people and creates obstacles to economic growth and development. It is of primary importance that the issue of the economic impact of the digital divide be tackled for an efficient and sustainable economic progression.

The most visible and the immediate economic impact of the digital divide is witnessed in the sector of employment. Today, for almost all kinds of jobs, the ability to access the internet as well as digital literacy are basic prerequisites. For those individuals particularly from low income households and remote areas who cannot access the Internet nor own a digital device, the digital divide tends to restrict and hinder their employability. The digital divide, which reinforces unemployment and underemployment, further deepens the general economic disparities.

The rise of e-commerce and the gig economy not just that highlight the economic disturbance of the digital divide. The COVID-19 pandemic has not only accelerated digital transformation but has also brought the urgency of digital skills and reliable internet connectivity into sharp focus for businesses. Workers who are not digitally connected find themselves in a state that such job positions might be far from them as they cannot participate in remote opportunities. Additionally, the gig economy with a greater dependence on digital details is not for those without digital access since they are not benefited from it and they cannot join the economic field.

Small and medium-sized enterprises (SMEs) are heavily affected by the digital divide. These businesses represent about 90% of all enterprises and are the main source of employment, but many of them have challenges to digitally compete because they possess a lack of Digital Identity. Furthermore, it is confirmed with the absence of digital technologies, that are the reason most businesses to fail at the commencement of trade either over the internet or other onscreen channels. Those businesses that don't have high-speed internet or digital assistive technologies will not grasp wider markets. They will not also be able to do electronic business. There is also no possibility for them to be more creative and innovators, which are the main hindrances to digital inclusion of SMEs.

Education and skills development, fundamental elements for the achievement of economic growth, are also significantly handicapped by the digital divide. Digital learning has made Google Classroom and other virtual learning platforms very accessible. These tools are beneficial to an educator as they deliver classes and help students improve assignments. However, pupils who are unable to attend school are taught through them, making them backward and unable to have technology incorporated into their educational experience. This educational discrepancy translates into a workplace-skill deficit and the shortage of workers having qualifications needed for the job and can also slow down economic development. Funding digitals tools in the field of education and teaching computer skills are great ways to visualize and build a professional workforce.

The digital divide is also important in the provision of financial services, which are today mostly carried via digital platforms. Digital financial inclusion is one of the most effective ways to give the poor and unbanked access to payment and credit systems, insurance, and investment. The inability to use digital transaction tools can leave an individual or business in various unfavorable situations like inability to open savings accounts, lack of access to credit, and an inability to acquire or sell off economic goods without the direct legal support of an intermediary. All of the financial exclusion results in an accumulation of inequality and limits the circle of economic mobility, especially in regions of developing countries which are not fully equipped with traditional banking facilities.

One such area is the field of healthcare, the line of business whose development and stability has a direct impact on the state's economy. A concept of based and developed on digital divide has been revealed is the health system. All healthcare entities are tied to these new concepts, which economically and functionally depend on the internet. Telehealth and digital health services are important cost-effective solutions for this kind of medicine especially in remote and rural areas. The promise and potential of Digital Health can be realized only when Digital Divide is eradicated. Those who are digitally disconnected will not be able to utilize telehealth services. Even the call center can't solve this and you may come to know your file by snail mail.

Another economic aspect of the digital divide is a matter dealing with rural development and urbanisation. Rural areas, which are often lacking in digital infrastructure, are more backward due to numerous reasons. Further, there is displacement because the absence of digital connections limits economic opportunities in these areas. METHODOLOGY: The research design that will be used for this study is a descriptive survey. This kind of design demands the description of the behavior of the respondent and the correspondents. Since factors that affect the social and economic development of the rural area are not dominating, the cities have expanded instead of running down. That in turn results in the depopulation of the countryside which will further lead to regional economic disparities because of the underdevelopment of rural areas and overcrowding of urban areas. However, investment in the development of rural digital infrastructure can surprisingly make those areas economically active.

On the other hand, the public sector's effectiveness and the delivery of public services is under the influence of digital inequality, this based on the -government partnership, and not only the level of digital readiness and access to the channels. The digital era is growing so fast and government is using digital platforms providing services, disciplining people, and also showing accountability in governance. Despite this, the population of people who do not have an internet connection is excluded from government services, which prevents them from participating in governance and getting public services. This disconnecting factor can be associated with a lack of trust in government reflected in the low involvement of citizens in civic engagement. These actions are detrimental to the stability of a society as well as obstruct economic growth. So, prevailing digitalization in government services by ensuring objectivity, transparency, and integrity is a take-off point for the process of inclusive governance and setting the grounds for sustainable economic development.

Going about the process of mitigating the economic effects of the digital divide comprises different components. The viability of digital infrastructure and investments in rural and other underserved regions are important due to increased demand for accessible internet data traffic. Public-private partnerships bring resources and skills and can make real the manufacturing of these products and infrastructure maintenance. Moreover, there are pertinent methods that policy makers can propose to work on. For instance, the intervention of the state by reducing the cost of internet services and digital devices is facilitated by policies that promote affordability. Additionally digital devices can help in the digital learning process to enable the students to have a taste of the digital world.

Steps for digital literacy training and hatching apprentices are yet another critical component of narrowing the digital divide. School authorities, along with community organisations, join hands with politicians to provide training and resources that help people master the digital skills necessary for the modern economy. This covers not only in the aspect of learning how to use digital devices but also trying to improve the last more expeditious skills like coding, data analysis, even cybersecurity.

ICT sector should give priority to the development of systems and services that are accessible and useable by everyone, irrespective of their abilities or the environment they are living in. This implies user-friendly designs, the use of assistive technologies for the people with disabilities, and also creating content in diverse different languages. Alongside designing a digital environment, the inclusion of all individuals will help to increase the number of users in the digital industry.

To address the imposing global levels, international cooperation also plays a pivotal role. Digital access discrepancy is not a country-specific issue but a global issue. Uneven development participates in digital inequality differently for different countries. The global disparities in internet access have the deficient for developed countries and underdeveloped countries alike, but the underdeveloped countries stand a bigger chance to have the negative effects. This is particularly essential because some of the international organizations are going to use technology. This is essential as institutions of different categories are going to make use of technology. It is only when organizations give and take knowledge, distribute information, and create the environment of best tweaking of the technology that underprivileged communities and social groups of peoples have the possibility to close these gaps. One of the other most important conditions is to create this access to technology on a global basis, as it can promote social development and offer more opportunities to poor people.

Primary focus on the economic consequences of the digital divide is essential for the enhancement of a more feasible, inclusive, and effective digital economy. Adopting technology is not the only way out for the development of countries where human being is struggling with diseases, skin poverty, and illiteracy. The only tool to solve this problem is the all-out help of the developed world.

Another way to encourage people to utilize the digital economy is with the use of technology, which enables such people to enjoy the convenience of cyber financial dealings. This regulation would be impossible without using digital technologies. Consequently, this would enhance equality in labour relations for all social groups from a professional perspective.

Solutions to Bridge the Divide

The digital divide, the gap between those who have access to digital technologies and those who do not, poses significant barriers to achieving social and economic justice in the modern world. As digital technologies increasingly become part of various parts of life in education, medicine, working, and the participation in society, the need for digital inclusion is becoming more urgent. The issue may be solved with forming public and private partnerships on different levels as well as guarantying that the whole growth happens in a transparent way. Overcoming this has a broader approach including improving infrastructure, affordability, raising digital literacy, as well as putting in place policies that promote inclusiveness.

The development of digital infrastructure is one of the most essential solutions to bridging the digital divide. A high-quality broadband connection is the core of digital inclusion, and yet many rural and underserved areas still do not have access to broadband with a high-speed. By combining efforts, countries or regions can effectively invest in the data carriage system necessary for all regions to have a reliable, speedy internet network. A public-private partnership method can be one of the best ways to combine the financial and human resources which in turn will lead to the fast and low-cost deployment of the needed network in areas that are not typically profitable to serve. Furthermore, schemes such as bringing internet via satellite technology and using community networks offer the needed interactivity to users in out-of-the-way places.

Affordability appears to be another essential component. This means affordability of internet and digital devices. The Internet and digital gadgets' cost is very high. Without affordability also, the other solutions won't be successful. Affordability is important and in reality, many low-income families are not in a position to pay for the full cost of internet service or digital instruments. To address this, the presence of policies that advocate maximum affordability and reduce prices is critical. In the eyes of many families, this is what makes them shun the presence of these technologies. Therefore, it is only possible to encourage competition among internet service providers to bring down prices and provide high-quality services. Similarly, giving tax incentives or grants to companies that can offer such telecommunication services at a lower rate is also an alternative way to make the technology more accessible.

Differentiating, digital literacy stands as a vital part of digital inclusion. Possessing technology without the means to use them is the same as not having it. Starting from basic computer skills and finishing with the ability to evaluate digital content, digital literacy involves a number of competences. It is then essential for schools and other learning establishments to include digital literacy into their set courses while introducing this curriculum from the early educational stages. At the same time, non-profit organizations can propose digital literacy workshops to the adults, especially those from the most disadvantaged regions, and these actions will ensure they become legitimate digital societies members. These programs should involve both teaching and assistance, thus helping the individual to take full control of the digital world regarding normal practices such as communication, research, and social networks.

The same applies to the inclusive design principles, which are a must for ensuring the digital technologies are available to, accessible to, and usable by all. Digital platforms and services, therefore, should be designed in a way that they provide for the diverse needs of the different users, including people with disabilities. To solve this problem, designers may include low-level user interfaces, provide content in many different ways, and incorporate assistive technology in this process. By considering utility and drag-and-drop features in engineering, technology developers can maintain a stable and convenient environment that is easy to all of its users.

Public policy is another element to play in filling the digital inclusion gap. Policymakers should stand up for digital inclusion as a chief goal in their agendas since recognition of digital access is fundamental in participation in different spheres of social and economic life. At the central level the arrival of overall policies with a comprehensive action program that concerns infrastructure, affordability, literacy, and inclusivity is more relevant. They should also be based on statistical information and in-depth research that would enable them to target the specific interests of different communities." Additionally, accounts of the schemes to inculcate digital literacy should be flexible to respond to prodigy march in innovations.

International cooperation for conquering the international stage of digital knowledge and information has to be defined. This issue doesn't have the borders only of individual countries; it is the worldwide problems that concern different nations in a different way associated with their level of development. Collaboration between the countries, international organizations, and global tech firms would bring the knowledge, fund the application of specific best practices in the individual country's market and most importantly allocate the resources to fill the gap between digital haves and have nots. Projects like Sustainable Development Goals (SDGs) of the United Nations that cover fields such as digital inclusion can be used as a platform for international partnership and collective action.

Exerting a sense of responsibility for the part of the private sector is also developing the gap in the digital division. The technology sector should propose affordable high-tech products and invest in digital infrastructures, as well as provide training programs on digital technologies. Social investments aimed at encouraging access to digital tools are indispensable, especially when linked with public sector efforts. By pooling their resources and know-how, the corporate world can help to level the playing field digitally.

It's of primary importance to have community-based programs for breaking the digital divide. Local citizens are knowledgeable to a large extent about the local requirements and concerns of their place. Getting the community in the design and the execution of inclusion programs is the other way to make sure the interventions being performed would really be helpful and serve the purpose. Local community efforts, such as self-organized digital literacy programs or the founding of the community broadband connection, are also part of the solution with the holistic development of digital technologies.

For any country, the best way to eliminate the digital divide and ensure inclusive growth is through the use of technology. An ongoing research into digital exclusion can be of great help for analysts to better know about the roots of digital exclusion. And then develop a solution that suits the financial situation of the people.

Innovations in technology may help to make the situation better. Hence, by offering cheap devices, alternative connectivity options, and usable applications, you can give the user a lot of time to fusion with modern technology. You can also simply encourage research and innovations by making funding available, by helping business people form partnerships and by joining in collaborations with innovators and project teams.

What one has to understand is that to bridge this gap is a very hard and continuous task of many parts which cannot be accomplished without the participation of government, the private sector, learning institutions, local communities, and international communities. To be able to support a digital divide mindful society, these entities should join forces to come up with effective and realistic policies. Social inclusion should be realized through bridging the digital divide especially in its four areas of terminal availability, of internet costs, literacy, and lastly, inclusivity. This balanced approach will be the medium through which global disparities will be reduced and a sense of unity will be created.

Ethical Design and Regulation

"Design is not just what it looks like and feels like. Design is how it works." — Steve Jobs

Digital technologies have been making inroads into our personal and social spheres, and the demand for ethical design and regulation is quite understandable. The development of digital technologies and the framework of rules and guidelines governing their behavior often bring about important societal changes; from infringement of personal security and privacy to issues of equity and justice. This section dwells on the principles of ethical design and the role of regulatory work in setting effective guardrails to make sure that technology plays an important role as a common good and at the same time be the protector of fundamental rights.

It is a clear characteristic of ethical design to use well-based foundations that aim at entities and users of digital artifacts and systems. This is recurring throughout the enunciation of technology's suitability to one user and the whole of society, followed by the stages of design. Ethical design goes beyond morphologically aesthetic and functional; it features the sound philosophical and ethical basis of technological development. Included are transparency, privacy, inclusiveness, and accountability. It is through the inclusion of these values by means of the design process, as presented above, that the technology can safeguard the rights of the users, and hence form the basis of trust and the encouragement of responsible use.

It is through regulation that the digital environment finds its shape and justice prevails. Good practice and principle-based regulation make sure that technological advancements are not made misusing ethical considerations. Legal frameworks are needed to prevent abuse, protect consumer rights, and maintain fair competition in the digital marketplace. Regulatory-wise, multiple aspects can be handled at once like privacy by data, cyber security, and ethical practice using AI. However, regulation should equally be mutually informed, i.e., embracing innovation without leaving behind societal interests that it aims to protect.

Ethical design and regulatory ethics pose significant constraints on the pace at which technology is rapidly advancing. The digitization of industries through AI, machine learning, and data analytics is paving the way for the creation of new opportunities and the transformation of existing industries, nonetheless, they also introduce new ethical issues. A good example would be gender bias or racial bias, which AI systems will perpetuate by various means of bias in training data, thus resulting in partial risk for discriminative decisions. Ethical design and the functionality of ethical technologies rely deeply upon the fair, trustworthy, and accountable nature of this approach and the transparency impetus that drives the regulatory oversight.

A feature that is also crucial in ethical design is inclusivity. Digital technologies should be available and affordable to individuals who irrespective of their abilities, socio-economic level, or geographic location. Inclusivity manifests itself as products or systems that are robust and usable by any potential user, reaching inclusivity requirements and thus providing an opportunity to expand digital equality. Some examples that involve a broad range of users are making easy-to-use interfaces with or providing these impaired users with the most technologically advanced technologies and exploring the individual issues the over-represented sectors deal with.

The are lawful provisions that ensure data protection in cyberspace, and privacy in particular is one of the most ancient and inviolable forms of rights. Successful ethical design practices should naturally promote the right of privacy among users by ensuring that choices are under the control of individuals. This can be ensured through methods like encryption of the data, offering clear and simple privacy settings as well as being transparent regarding the data collection and use practices. As this effort takes a form of standardisation and close examinations to being the right course of action for the data protection issue, Privacy Regulations are the complementary features that just like the building blocks, lay the foundation supporting that as well as homing in the fact that organisations should always be responsible about any privacy violations.

By having absolute transparency and accountability, a digital system can visibly promote trust. These tools should operate using processes that we are all familiar with and the true nature of what your data is being used for should always come out. Simple communication and user education controlled through ethical design practices can lead towards informed and approved consent of individuals about their digital interactions. In addition, the regulatory framework will be beneficial to impose these key components regarding the realization of the data protection laws and the data security regulations this mere concept of cybersecurity deals with. Moreover, it will make mandatory that various institutions disclose and report the privacy risks that their information systems may possess, provide obligations to implement security measures redirecting therefore a more privacy-aware culture, and establish procedures for monitoring and control to force organizations to be transparent in the implementation of the code and be responsible for the consequences.

This topic is going to be based on the examination of the fundamental principles of ethics in design and the active role which regulation plays in the growth of responsible technology. The discussion will be around not only the description of cases of well-implemented ethical design but also an inquiry about how useful the regulatory framework might be when looking at existing examples of such frameworks and some more that are yet to come. Meanwhile, we will take a look at a number of case studies of successful ethical design practices detailed by examining different technologies, review the different ways in which the regulatory framework is being enforced and develop a strategy for how we can handle arising issues with better design practices. Through these explorations, we endeavor to demonstrate that including ethical considerations in the development and oversight of digital technologies is nonnegotiable. They should help in equal dissemination of these technologies in the society remaining entirely ecological and respecting all its members, ensuring that they empower the individual agent in the society.

Principles of Ethical Design

The extensive development of digital technologies has reshaped the configuration of human interaction, communication, and productivity. As these technologies are deeply woven with the societal fabric, the importance of ethical design has reached its climax. Ethical design does not only pertain to the aspects of functionality and aesthetics but has more to do with creating technologies that are not only respectful but also more human-enriched in a way. Technology will then be at the service of people for people. In this article, we feature the principles of ethical design and highlight how these principles can be implemented in practice through technology development that focuses on people's wellbeing and rights.

At the core of ethical design lies the principle of user-oriented design. It is essential for ethical design that people are at the heart of it. User-centric design implies that technology is designed to serve, firstly and mainly, the interests and needs of people who will be using it. The process of this design involves understanding in what ways diverse people can benefit from particular tech options and the technologists taking the lead in addressing them through an upfront interaction so they capture user feedback. A good technology, the user-centric design maintains, is one that is laconic in the interfaces but spry in the manner that helps advancing people's lives. One method is the iterative design approach involving several methods such as a series of tests, feedback, and improvement all based on observations from the actual users.

Transparency is yet another linchpin for ethical design. Users should be enlightened clearly about the functioning of the technology, the instances when the data is captured and how exactly the data is utilized. Transparent practice is no magic but a straight forward walking the talk. It encompasses the effective communication and disclousure step that consciously avoids any cunning or triky like approaches which only make things crystal clear for the curious mind leaving the technology to be used the way it is -- in a fully unethical manner. Privacy policies and terms of use in simple language should be published for, and understood by, every user. The open nature of information helps the users to gain the confidence on the side of the technology promoters, which promotes residual trust on the basis of being honest and truthful.

Nowadays privacy and data security are the most important principles of any ethically built product. In an era where data has become a valuable commodity, ensuring that user data remain confidential is crucial. One of the main elements of ethical design is the protection of personal data. It is about making sure that the content is appropriate for users' age, culture, and location by enabling particular security and privacy media. Security can be obtained by adopting encryption that has a key with a complicated format, and that is provided only to the authorized user. In addition, users can be allowed to edit their personal data, so they can fix data errors and remove the wrong data. They also should allow for the complete account removal and they must remove all the data from the data store.

Inclusivity is another important principle of ethical design. It's very important to have technology that everyone can access no matter what level you are at social, economical or geographically. This practice allows products and services to be naturally available to everyone because of personal excellence and especially technological innovation. Inclusive design facilitates the adaptation of the digital products and services to multiple user needs. Hence, the increased convenience of this approach allows room for broader access to assistive technology applications. In this case, adaptability to design is the only way to bring more people into the sphere of technology. This is achieved not only through the introduction of design modules that allow for the easy use of the products by disabled users but also in the design of the user interface in such a way that it accommodates the needs of all sorts of potential users.

Accountability stands for reliability in ethical design. The IT company and its developers cannot avoid the necessity of being responsible for the outcomes of their work. In this process, activated the remote wipe option on your device so that the information on it cannot be accessed by any means. Technical means include also the option to erase the information that is on the data volume and should happen when the device is lost. This also can involve info about the consent of the trusting third party to all data owners. Also, this will be a good option to hold the responsibility to the third parties. What should be mentioned and what is to be followed then, is that the issues of privacy raised can be solved only through ethics and a human change of view. The first should be the principle of honesty and the strong denunciation of the majority of hackers.

The fairness principle lies at the very heart of ethical design. Technologies must be built so that no matter what the user is equal, and for example, race, gender, or age is not taken into account, avoiding biases that may cause unfair treatment and, consequently, discrimination or exclusion. It is in particular effective with exemplar technologies such as AI and machine learning. Further, an AI algorithm that is programmed to reduce bias in society might be worsened to perpetuate it. Thats how it may happen due to naivety pretending that data collected on the field would be completely neutral. The aspect of achieving ethical design also includes preventive measures to detect and correct PIDs as well as abuse automation systems operating properly. Ethical design as far as that goes bridges the fault lines: the regularization of technological innovation as social justice and welfare, and the creation of a new model of user-centered society which, in turn, reduces digital oppression.

But the new tendency of sustainability has become ethical design so important. When you think about how much all that affects our analytical processing and our lives, the answer is simple. Digital literacy is high. Basically, we have a good chance of marrying technologies with the new literacy people will get. They may even get so good at using tech that they don't even need to be apple engineers.

Furthermore, it's important to be technology-driven by the principle of empowerment. Technology should be empowering the users, and the users should be provided with the tools, know-how, and the guidance they need for an in-demand digital lifestyle. This can be reached by creating technologies that convey user autonomy and guide through user-controlled ethical decision-making. Through designed empowerment, even limited resources like a short piece of a film or a manual for a device can be employed for the power of self-reliance. By empowering users, the ethical design lifestyle enables a sense of self-responsibility and self-esteem in the online world.

Collaboration and co-creation form the backbone of ethical design. Diverse participation in the design process comes through a multi-layered journey where users, experts, and community members are involved and add value to the creative process ensuring that a wide range of perspectives and needs are considered. Design practices involving cooperative interactions based on participative methods and respect for the input of all the players involved are common. The way this design is done will not only better the quality and relevance of the technological solutions but will also foster the feeling of own and common responsibility.

An ethical design is not like a single one concept but is an integrated approach consisting of the following features: user-centeredness, the open and plain idea of design, privacy, inclusivity, accountability, fairness, sustainability, empowerment, and collaboration. The principles on which these values are built are used to be the sources through which technology can be created and develop digital products and systems that are the champions of human dignity and well-being. As we keep on evolving, one of the agreed future prospects to ethics is the use of ethical design which will, in turn, keep evolving hand in hand with new technologies, and contribute positively to the society and cater to the responsibilities of ample individuals through the very quality of digitalization and its applications.

The Role of Designers and Engineers

The roles of designers and engineers are being valued more in today's fast-paced digital technology setup where they are concentrating on the betterment of their work processes. They are the ones who give life to the ever-evolving technology and make it and effective. However, in their often delicate relations with this same technology, they are also the guardians of the ethical bounds and the ethical guardians of the technology meant to serve the society. As the pushers of boundaries, they are the co-creators together with technology, where they both give blessing to how well technology influences human beings.

These professions shouldn't be kept on the back bench for the redesign of the digital platform and the creation of sophisticated software and their functionality. There isn't the case when the two roles can differ. After all, they are also accountable for setting norms and standards that differentiate technology from the things that are not considered to be human and environmentally unfriendly.

Engineers and designers create good fail safe systems, thus rendering life more easy for the human being. They are at the beginning of the creation of new technologies by taking the initially exposed ideas and making them dead right products and services. Their involvement aims at opening doors for greater users' space. Their work starts by uncovering the real needs and wishes of the buyers which gives rise to a unique product that is both here and able to be adapted. The designers' mantra to keep the user at the front is the architecture, involving them from the outset and it leads to excellent products.

Designers and engineers symbolize the philosophy of belonging to the equation of social progress. Socially inclusive technology is the real thing which means that technology leaves the creators with no lives and gets integrated into the lives of the society. This implies the process of including understanding various elements of diversity such as but not limited to physical and cognitive abilities, economic and cultural environments. Inclusive design is not just about the expansion of usability database, but more so equalizing the playing field, allowing everyone the opportunity to use the same tools as well as becoming an identity based on inalienable rights of humans. In the modern digital age, each person is granted the right to use technology, and further still, anybody can be involved in its creation.

Reflecting the fact that ethical considerations are one of the most important aspects of the work carried out by designers and engineers. The choices made during the design and the development process may have serious repercussions, threatening privacy, security, and user freedom. For instance, when developing software that collects personal data, engineers have to ensure that they include robust security features to protect the data from unauthorized access and abuse. Designers are also expected to provide full details to the users on how their data will be utilized, thus, promoting transparency and trust. But this ethical responsibility also applies not only to facing the potential biases that can lurk in algorithms and preventing technology from becoming a tool of perpetuation and enhancement of existing iniquities.

Another important aspect of the work carried out by designers and engineers is sustainability. Much like the rest of the world in its quest to beat the environment, the technological sector also has to resort to sustainable practices. It involves the development of products that are environmentally harmless, made from renewable materials, and are energy efficient. Engineers have numerous techniques at their disposal to fight electronic waste, for example, the creation of detachable consumer electronics that can be quickly repaired or replaced. Awareness that companies, working through their design teams and engineers, must actively lead green technology movements and contribute to environmental sustainability.

Collaboration lies at the core of the occupation of creators and engineers. The advancements in modern technology have raised the stakes for multidisciplinary teamwork, which recruits talents from different disciplines to tackle the different challenges. Designers as intermediary messengers between the engineers and artists have to work in sync so that they can visually capture their innovative ideas artistically but also the projects can function as prototypes. Not to mention that collaboration with the community, such as users, business people, and policymakers, is important in the process of research and development of new technology that is both socially and economically relevant.

Technological evolution implies constant learning and adapting.

Keeping up with all the novelties in their industry demands that designers and engineers are continually updating their knowledge and mastering new skills. In other words, it is a commitment of the lifetime to learn forever and not shrink from the changes taking place in one's profession. However, as technological advancements become a reality so also does the definition and solutions to ethical problems linked to technology. They are the ones expected to take initiatives to methodically address new ethical issues that emerge with the development and use of these technologies. IE Robotics & NLP companies have been around for a few years and they have made great steps on the front of real-life implementation, however, the process of speaking with computers is still not perfect or can at least be improved.

Designers as well as engineers take part not only in the creation of specific items but also more broadly into shaping the technological space as a whole. Consequently, they have the opportunity to set the bar for other companies and shape the rules for how technology is made and employed worldwide. They see this process as an ethical obligation and at the same time set targets that should be achieved in the present as well as in the future. These ideas should coincide with that what is good for humanity. Ethical design in technology should also be legislated for by designers and engineers.

Control of personal development belongs to formal education for designers and engineers. Educational institutions are mandated to provide intellectual resources and the morality-related part of all fields of knowledge. A coherent approach in education not only produces well-respected citizens but it also assists professionals-in-the-making in managing the complex environment of technology. Curricula that combine the ethics of moral construction, recycling, and diversity in the learning process guide learners through the common rationale for ecological doings and the sense of righteousness that they impart.

The new message for staying in the company comes from the work of designers and engineers, championing user-centric design principles, and ethical design principles. In addition to these, they participate in the successful implementation of new concepts (22). This gives priority to the Social Responsibility and Public Welfare Culture.

Designers and engineers have an influence that stretches across the entire world and influence international undertakings where their achievements might address numerous problems humanity is facing, which include healthcare accessibility and climate change mitigation. The potential to resolve global problems of health and climate change lies also in the possibility to develop new projects through crowdfunding and financings.

The role of designers and engineers is versatile and ongoing. This as well includes the design part not only in terms of their project management abilities but also actual ethical responsibilities and the promotion of sustainable technologies in the world. They have to face the delicate path of culture and therefore have to be the bad boys of the organization.

Regulation in the Tech Industry

Technology has rebuilt the living world by bringing in vast modifications with the introduction of new potentials and process improvements. A reverse side of the coin to cherish the widespread technological advancements is the necessity to cope with various challenges – which would require a lot of policy-level changes and decisions. This thing is because the major task of this industry is to set rules, which regulate the interaction between the industry and its customers, not forgetting to provide a productive ground for the industry players. To cope up with the challenges of the internet age, a policy should be designed that solves the problems but also encourage the innovative environment to keep enhancing and fulfil accountability for the usage of the new tech-advancements.

A primary reason for technology industry regulation is to secure consumer rights, as well as personal data. The growth of digital technology on one hand resulted in the collection and processing of large amounts of personal data. The innovation and rapid user acceptance of those services' benefits notwithstanding, a set of commercial- and also privacy-related issues also is emerging. When security breaches and cases of personal information abuse are on the rise, this clearly indicates the urgent need for regulations that offer such data protection. Apart from this, The General Data Protection Regulation of the European Union guarantees consumers those rights and specifies the necessary conditions and responsibilities of data privacy and information protection, and thus puts in place a globally high standard for data protection.

Another matter that stands out with regulation is that it guarantees fair competition within the industry. The concern about unfair competition and market concentration that can be caused by big tech companies like the so-called 'Big Tech' brought strict regulations on multiple records. Some of the organizations that receive more criticism are Microsoft, Google, and Facebook, and in addition, they stay most of the time within sight of the Secretary of the Navy especially over the issue of advocating the "Big Tech" dominancy over the whole market platform. These regulations prevent companies from proceeding towards monopolies, making the competition severe and encouraging new companies to emerge. The antitrust investigations and court cases which exclude those technological goliaths illustrate that only a thorough framework of regulation has the power to maintain a win-win game for the market and protect the customer's rights.

Regulatory oversight is also an essential idea because ethical concerns start growing with increasing AI.

The application of AI technologies complicates industries in healthcare, finance, medical and other fields; however, it raises severe ethical issues. Aspects such as racial prejudice, transparency, and accountability are crucial AI questions. Unbalanced elements can cause and even increase social disparities, affecting directly to the processes of work and management, and indirectly to hiring, lending, and judicial areas. One of the functions of regulation is to determine the standards that developers and the AI industry should meet safe, transparent, and legally accountable AI practices.

Cyber-fraud prevention is another domain where rules must be followed. As online technologies are more deeply integrated into critical infrastructure and daily activities, the risk of falling for a cyberattack rises. Cyber crashes could directly lead to severe disruptions of services by local utilities and vital services. Sometimes, it might cause a cybersecurity incident which can lead to the loss of information. Furthermore, such a situation is transformed, causing one time events to make buildings unusable for a long time. Regulations that are referring to strong cybersecurity measures, regular audits, and incident reporting are methods to boost the resistance of digitized systems. They will make sure that organizations apply restricted cybersecurity policies and adopt security procedures against existing cyber threats.

Intellectual property (IP) rights are a significant concern in the tech area as well. To encourage the introduction of modern technologies and financial backing of innovative ideas, providing IP protection is a must. Nonetheless, the speeded up development of technologies seems to complicate the classic IP frameworks. Patents, copyrights, and trademarks must evolve to address new issues like noetic patents, open-source development, and digital content distribution. Meanwhile, authorities must make a decision concerning the extent of protecting the intellectual property rights and supporting collaboration and innovation.

One more subject that requires to regulate is the relationship between job and the technology and its impact on the employment and the labor market. The workforce is becoming different and the effect of it sandwiches the whole society. Labor Market regulation can help to diminish its inhumane face by helping the workforce to adapt and be re-staffed with e.g. new sets of skills. It shows that sharing the benefits of tech advances widely among the people is absolutely necessary if we want to sustain social harmony and economic development.

The areas like environment that are caused by the technologies are coming up and they hence need a strategy for regulation. E-waste and emissions of CO2 result from creating, using and dumping digital devices. In the networked society, environmental sustainability is better seen through policies providing sustainable living, eco-friendly technologies, and the reutilization of resources. The development of the environment can be taken in hand with regulators who are to focus on developing more sustainable digital economy.

Nothing but the solidarity among cultures around the world can make an effective regulation possible in the tech industry. Digital technologies are a global issue and that is why international experts are working on a solution to that problem. They are jointly responsible for global issues such as data protection, cybersecurity, and antitrust and they need to work together to construct policies that would address these challenges. The international organisations together, such as the United Nations and the World Trade Organization, are supposed to stimulate countries to initiate the cooperation, thereby making it possible to build frameworks that are acceptable for all globally despite the cross-border character of the problems.

The significance of the tech industry's self-regulation needs to be acknowledged. Making good use of these principles and practices is just as crucial to industry regulation and can also help maintain fairness and good behavior. Integrating technology companies might do it, for example, by observing rules of conduct, being transparent and keeping ethics, to signal to all their stakeholders that the companies have a good foundation in digital innovation. One of the outcomes of this cooperation will be the appearance of the regulatory surroundings flexible and effective which will be able to tailor its rules responding to the fast development of technology while taking into account the needs of the society.

One of the key elements of good regulation is indeed education and public awareness. As digital technologies become more pervasive, it is vital that consumers give a clear picture of the owner of their digital data and the impact that one can have on automated technologies. Awareness activities will help the individuals become smart, sensorial social actors, be careful in their personal interactions, and examine all the channels. The public could also be involved by the regulators to ensure transparency and to foster inclusiveness and trust in the people and organizations involved directly in the application of the legal measures.

The regulation of the tech industry is a multifaceted process with various scopes and applications that keep changing with the development of the technology itself. Checking the rights of the users, ensuring a fair competition environment, addressing the issues of ethics ad cybersecurity, and supporting ecological balance are some of the key blocks of comprehensive regulatory systems that aim to balance the need for innovation and the principle of accountability through regulatory support for the tech industry to show that it's both dynamic and responsible. This view, despite any disadvantages it may have, will generate a more prosperous existence since there will be forces to keep authorities in check and moral standards to stay high.

Ethical Standards and Guidelines

The rapid evolution of digital technologies and artificial intelligence (AI) has catalyzed a wave of profound changes across various industries like healthcare and finance, as well as education and entertainment. However, this explosive growth has to be addressed ethically, imposing the need for robust ethical standards and guidelines. These are crucial tools for making sure that the technological progress is not only in line with the society's ethos but also channels itself towards the common good. Descriptions of ethical standards and guidelines as the foundation of responsible innovation guiding developers, companies, and policymakers in the creation and deployment of technology.

Ethical standards in technology are a comprehensive set of rules created with claims concerning issues ranging from privacy, transparency, fairness, and accountability. Privacy is a profound human right that digital age must not constrain. Although technology is brought in by the continuous collection and research of enormous user data, privacy protection becomes a top priority. Ethical guidelines for data privacy are meant to take care of the issue of obtaining informed consent from users, data security ensuring, and giving control to individuals over their personal information. These are strategies that ensure privacy in the way of creating relationships of trust between users and providers of digital services as well as building feelings of security and trust within digital platforms.

Furthermore, transparency defines one of the crucial ethical criteria in technology. Users must be told about how technology works, the data is collected, and what is being done with it. Transparent design strategies require of a fair and transparent communication and be freed from manipulations and other dishonest behavior. For example, privacy policies and terms of service must be formulated in plain language in order to make them accessible and easily understood to all the users. Transparent processes lead to technology providers' credibility and user trust in the companies leading to co-working and being legally responsible.

It is critical to ensure fairness in the development and deployment of AI systems according to ethical standards. AI offers the opportunity to significantly revolutionize various aspects of society; at the same time, the technology exposes itself to significant risks when it is used unsustainably. One of the most critical ethical issues related to artificial intelligence is to be delivered documentation of where biased algorithmic training, either intentional or not, causes unjust or discriminatory outcomes. The guidelines for AI development and the ethical requirements have come to the fore due to the unfairness of the data used, they are very strict on the issues, such as the method of forming diverse and representative datasets, the implementation of bias detection and mitigation strategies and the regulation of AI systems by regular audits and evaluations. Fairness is a paramount requirement since fairness promotes equity and justice in the AI systems {but not the etymology in the system? what is AI} that they develop, whereas by this way, they would mitigate current inequalities.

Accountability is a crucial element in the technology area of ethical standards. TAll developers and companies that create technologies will be responsible for the outcomes they bring to the end-users and society as a whole. The targets can be achieved only by performing an impact assessment that offers a comprehensive view of the vulnerabilities and the potential dangers and then adopting preventive measures to avert them. Moreover, another effort is the transparency of the decision-making process and the readiness to give access to external influence. Furthermore, when new issues present themselves, companies should be ready to take ownership and resolve them in a fast and effective manner, making it to clear that abiding by moral aims is crucial and user trust is a must.

Ethical standards and guidelines are not immutable; they must respond to new challenges and developments in technology. Being in the state of a dynamic environment in the tech sector requires a balanced ethical approach that provides for continuity and adaptation. The vital thing is to engage all actors among them - users, experts and members of the public in developing these ethical guidelines which are going to be suitable and have been tried and tested. In doing so, stakeholders from different walks of life, such as users, specialists as well as local community members, must be brought in to participate in the substantiation and effectiveness of the ethical rules. Ethical activities in the collective approach to ethics are a guarantee that different sets of perspectives and.

The Asilomar AI Principles stands as one of the glaring instances of ethical AI, initiated by the Future of Life Institute in 2017. They present a wide-ranging discussion of AI technology ethics encompassing essential issues such as scientific research, societal impact etc. They are specifically focusing on the AI which appears to be transparent, accountable and above all helpful. For example, the European Union's Ethics Guidelines for Trustworthy AI provide a comprehensive framework for ethical AI development and deployment. Seven main requirements for trustworthy AI such as human agency and oversight, technical robustness, privacy and data governance, transparency, diversity and fairness, societal well-being, and accountability, were presented in the guidelines.

Professional organisations and industry bodies have a crucial role in this effort, setting high ethical standards and guidelines. Organizations like IEEE and ACM, other than the already mentioned one, have also embraced the notion by adopting codes of ethics and professional policies as the framework for their members. These "codes" also accent the role of technology professionals to preserve the good and ethical use of technology as well as follow the public interest through their actions.

The provision of education and training is vital for the establishment of ethical standards in the technology industry. In the same way, higher learning institutions have to generate a system where pupils study morality integrated with the technology curriculum and not just learn the technical know-how. This will help students in understanding both the practices and morals at a time. Adult Learning or CPDs programs will also help fill emerging ethical gaps in the industry and keep pace by learning recent ethical practices.

Complementing ethical standards and guidelines enforcing corresponds to the role played of the Regulation. While the voluntary compliance to ethical standards is crucial, rules-based oversight and enforcement are crucial to ensure compliance. In this manner, the General Data Protection Regulation (GDPR) from the European Union and other laws could be made use of to set clearly those standards of privacy and cybersecurity in legal terms but at the same time to make clear that companies should bear the responsibility of the protection of users' personal data. Regulatory agencies should establish the frameworks for ensuring that AI technologies are developed and implemented ethically, which can contribute to responsible and transparent use of these technologies.

Public knowledge and participation are the two cornerstones for the development of the ethical technology option. Informing the public about their rights and the ethical implications of technology gives the people freedom to take decisions and question the technology providers. The public discussion of ethical issues in technology paves the way for the society to demand higher standards and greater transparency, and it motivates companies to adhere to ethical standards.

The approval of ethical norms and standards turns out to be a critical factor in making technological advances serve society and not defy individual freedom. The practice of setting those principles such as well-defined privacy, transparency, fairness, and accountability, the tech sector can be filled with trust and assurance in their innovations. As technology advances, despite that they are still our partners and educators, and we cannot afford not to have regulators but to regulate and face new challenges. Thereby, we manage to control technology to operate for a positive outcome, bringing benefits of health and welfare to individuals and communities on a global scope.

The Future of Ethical Design

Technology is changing very quickly with artificial intelligence (AI), machine learning, and digital networking that has come forward as we also had predictions about such advancements. Because of this fast pace, the ethics of a technology field are more important than before. Ethical design allows technical innovation to follow societal values drive like justice, transparency, and responsibility. The future of ethical design will be based on its capability to adjust to new demands and utilize the opportunities and, in this, to make a technology world that is helpful to all.

The inclusion of the principle of the human being in the ethical design process is fundamental. Future developments in technology need to be based on what users would like to see and also respect their rights, instead of technological dominance over them. This involves design from a user's perspective. This is about creating technologies that take into account both the functional and non-material needs of people. In that way, they pure humanize the process of technology and make sense.

Transparency is another pillar of ethical design that will continue to influence the future. Because AI and other complicated technologies come into sight, the mechanisms of their working need to be understood more than ever. People should be able to make sense of these decisions by procedural explanations, figures showing which data was used, and expected influences that could happen if their technology was to be implemented. Future ethical design will probably involve approaches that are more sophisticated when taking the field of artificial intelligence into existence by involving the greater accessibility of machines and the trust gained in-novation.

Privacy scales are raised close to limitless heights given how digital technologies just seem to appear every day on the landscape. In future's discourse, the morality of design as it relates to digital technologies will be reminiscent of a concept that consists of personal data privacy, among which are differential privacy, homomorphic encryption, federated learning. These technologies are known to open doors for gaining insights from data as humans, however, without getting the data exposed to any possible misuse. Avoiding various risks by the unethical methods are set by a lot of purposes but the main one is generating efficiency and convenience cause these data should be protected using these technologies to ensure the individuals' private data security...

As the technology thrives out uplifting the inclusivity will stay as important as in the early days. The appearance of the technology means that it is necessary for all the human beings independently, they are disabled, or not native to technology, to be able to both enjoy and benefit from these technologies. The paradigm of future ethical design will need some revisions, which imply creating more and more inclusive interfaces, strengthening accessibility through tech and classically developed needs are met for different diversely marginal populations. Instead of that, equality and more user satisfaction are not only guaranteed but also are increased in numbers because the technology does not stop developing.

One of the main ethical issues and possibilities of AI technology is the ethical use of AI. Artificial intelligence is a growing potential partner for human beings but it also represents a hazard to society if it is not carefully developed and implemented. Future ethical design will need to address issues such as algorithmic bias, accountability, and the ethical implications of autonomous systems. This is done by implementing not only technical recommendations but also the ethical guidelines which keep in mind how AI devices should be produced and used.

One positive step toward addressing the problem should be the establishment of AI principles. The IEEE and the European Union have already kicked off this work, not very long ago, but nicer future projects will require a more all-inclusive approach and also the possibility of doing it on a global scale. They must place checks and balances all through AI development, ranging from the raw data to model training, to provision of the service, followed by monitoring. In addition, technology manufacturers can show the way for a green AI that reflects human rights and pursues public good by setting up unambiguous technical regulations.

Another critical need for ethical designing of the future is considering sustainability. With the environmental consequences of technology significantly increasing, the focus of designers and engineers will shift towards sustainable innovation. It means using energy-efficient tools, recycling unused electronics, and creating products with prolonged life cycles. An additional, revised approach to ethical design will likely include an expansion of the circularity concept of economy, which implies that products are specifically designed with reuse, refurbishing, and recycling in mind.

Ethical design must also look at the broader social impact of technology. This would entail examining how robotics impacts employment, education as well as social relations. With the rise of automated work and AI, ethical technology would need to use modern technology alongside social skills, providing new opportunities for employment. Furthermore, in education, ethical design can guarantee the availability of assistive digital tools that will contribute to learning, regardless of learners' socio-economic status.

The future of ethical design will be shaped by regulation. A comprehensive framework for proper ethical codes will need to be put in place by governments, as well as national and international organizations, in order to ensure that tech firms are forced to operate ethically. Law will be used to protect privacy, secure data, and forestall monopolistic practices. Besides the implementation of the laws the regulations should be styled in a way to keep pace with the rapid technology trends. The role of the governing bodies will be the mainstay as it needs a collective effort among the supervisors and academia in the setting up of the regulatory frameworks.

The significance of public awareness and the importance of education will also be necessary in the future of ethical design. It is very important that everyone learns how it works and to be conscious of its impact on society as the technology evolves. This should be done not entirely through formal education but also through public awareness campaigns, and facilitated resources to build a deeper understanding of technology. The tech-industry customers will be assisted by the users' skill to face this industry accountably with information. They will have to be able to make personal choices and know how to access data as a society with access to both old and new technologies if they are well-informed about the advantages and risks involved.

Interdisciplinary research is crucial for the improvement of ethical design. The new technological threat is not one-dimensional and thus the various areas of science need to be brought together to tackle it. Among such disciplines are computer science, ethics, law, sociology, and psychology which provide a perspective of broad-based and diverse culture to the problems at hand. Ethical design will be more focused on interdisciplinary teams. The provision of diverse thinking and synergy will have an impact on complex problems and innovative ways of solving them. The inclusive approach allows all at all stages in technology evolution to consider ethical obligations as a foundation.

Elevation being a necessity for an efficient result, it gets easier with the application of the ethical design which evolves and adapts to change but never neglects its core value. Paring down user-centricity, privacy, and sustainability, the interdisciplinary collaboration also sometimes proves to be the best foundation for the mastermind of a digital era. Technology can be increased beyond the capacity of data. However, the human mental, emotional, and spiritual experience of daily life remains basically unchanged. At the same time, while privacy, human rights, transparency, AI ethics, tokenized legislation, and ethical design will continue to be debated, some international collaborations at the U.N. could help keep the global internet accessible and open.

Environmental Ethics and Technology

"The Earth does not belong to us: we belong to the Earth." – Marlee Matlin

In the ongoing phase, society has not resolved the immense issues such as climate change, resource depletion and environmental degradation. There has been a great meeting between technology and environmental ethics over the last decades. The technology-ethics dynamic finds its reflection in Peter Singer, who argues that the intersections of human beings, animals, and machines in the contemporary setting call for attention to moral responsibilities.

In this chapter, we aim to look at both sides of the coin in the relationship between technological progress and the human species' impact on the environment. While the advent of green technologies involves more advanced applications like reducing the amount of harmful gases, it also entails the use of eco-friendly alternatives to conventional materials. To operate responsibly with these new technologies we need to think about ethics and social responsibility further. The practices of environmental ethics, essential in promoting more sustainable practices through technology, are necessary for turning progress in the digital age into one that is beneficial to the health and sustainability of the planet.

Invention of new technology can lead to positive environmental outcomes. Renewable energy technologies like solar and wind power provide sustainable alternatives to hot-burning porridge, making it possible to reduce the amount of greenhouse gases and, concomitantly, to control global warming. Revolution in energy storage methodology and smart grid technologies are able to improve energy and resource efficiency in renewable energy systems; thereby, a more sustainable energy infrastructure is thus an encouragement. Furthermore, precision farming technologies are making our food systems more efficient because they use water, fertilizers, and pesticides more frugally, which results in the implementation of low environmental impact agricultural practices and the saving of natural habitats.

Contrary to popular belief, all technology has damaging ecological consequences. While it is true that technology brings many environmental benefits, paradoxically, technology produces environmental diseases and hazards that are varied and numerous. The process of manufacturing electronic devices involves the extraction of raw materials, leading to habitat destruction and major environmental crises in a number of cases. In addition, the electricity created for the power needs of the production of these instruments along with their function deepens the problem of C emissions and global ecology. Likewise, e-waste which is also termed as electronic waste is another dangerous issue whereby harmful materials can spill out into the environment from the disposed of devices and in this way soil and water can get virtually contaminated.

Issues like the fact that technology is a kind of two-edged sword—that is, it can offer a cure and, at the same time be a problem for the environment too—help us understand why providing environmental education and information is crucial in today's technological world. Overhead is representing by the company making recurring security, identity, and virus protection payments to an outsource supplier who is hosting the product and its data as well. Data Center can have a large footprint on energy consumption. One common problem of Internet-based activities is the use of up to 1850 watts according to studies. According to research, a typical computer needs to be built with approximately 240 units of energy in its production, involving a large range of electric systems, and, even if the economy's carbon emissions are lower, it still contributes to them, which is interesting.

What is the environmental cost of technology?

Running so many data centers can be responsible for environmental pollution. And mostly on data centers, which are cogwheels in the machinery of the digital economy, which are devourers of electricity doing the most. This kind of situation not only leads to carbon emissions but also to environmental degradation. To help with that, advances in energy-efficient computing like low-power processors and cooling equipment can reduce the carbon emissions produced by data centers. Also, companies can pledge to use renewable energy to the point of creating fewer needs based on planet resources. So these businesses fuel the change towards energy-sustainable infrastructure.

One other area the environment per Technological steps in is the supervision of the electronic waste. E-waste is the end result of the production, distribution, use, and disposal of EEE goods. The valuable resources are there in the waste to be upscaled and used again but if not properly managed could be very risky. Illegally doped e-waste and good working products from which commodities can be mined are to be targeted and carefully handled. Both tracking resources and production activities of the industrial sector and turning waste into resources with recycling systems that are efficient and not harmful can be used to address this challenge. While making products that are easy to be taken apart and recycled and also the infrastructure overlapping with e-waste make sure that the environmental repercussion of discarded electronic devices are minimized.

Environmental ethics also touch on technology's societal impacts. In addition to this, they bring to the table the positive societal effects of the technologically driven social reforms. For example, by helping a building or a transportation system be more efficiently used, AI can be helpful as a tool to save energy. And not only that, it can save waste in the production process and help a system be built of the means of controlling some of the hazards around nature. If the list is not taken into account, it could lead to the misuse of technology, such as automating homes with smart technologies, causing more energy consumption than before. Still, the benefit of this is marginal and the zero above risk.

This chapter will dig deep into these matters, then through the exploration, you will learn the ethical frameworks and practical strategies on integrating environmental ethics into technology development. As well as this, it will be presented the brief analysis of past initiatives and the research as well as specifying the obstacles and opportunities in the green area. The chapter also addresses the policy and regulation as they are essential tools that can capacitate eco-friendly technology practices in an iterative manner. This chapter will take you through themes including integration, ethics and computers and technology.

The Environmental Impact of Technology

Tremendous advances in technology have made life a lot easier, yet technology comes with disturbing concerns that are directly proportional to environmental issues. One of those concerns that the pros and cons of technology bring is the environmental factor of technology, which is multifaceted. The whole life cycle of digital devices and systems, starting from resource mining and production to use and disposal, is the environmental impact of technology so huge and varied it is unparalleled. Expansion of these issues is very important for saving the environment for our future generations so that technology can grow and not take the environment with it into extinction. People should be aware of these impacts besides addressing them. The success of such a process will create a situation where humans can live in harmony with technology which will be beneficial not only for human beings but also for the surroundings.

One thing, which stands out as a serious environmental problem because of technology, is the extraction of raw materials. For producing electronics, numerous raw materials are required. Here the basic raw materials are rare-earth metals, precious metals, and other minerals. Aggravating the situation, mining and processing these materials often engendered serious environmental woes such as habitat loss, soil and water pollution as well as drastic reduction in biodiversity. This can happen globally, for instance, cobalt mining, a primary raw material for a lithium-ion rechargeable battery, is known to be responsible for ecological destruction and human rights abuses in some locale.

The production of electronic devices also raises the issue of pollution. In the manufacturing of smartphones, laptops, and smartwatches, factories account for the largest to be blamed on the use of renewable resources and water, the production of waste and release of pollutants into the atmosphere. It is together with other environmental factors one can also mention hazardous chemicals used in the manufacture process, they pose additional health risk causing not only air and land pollution but also health issues for workers and residents around the plant. As increasingly more electronic devices find their way into our life, the demand for such devices will accelerate their existence while ecological imprint will multiply unless different eco-friendly production approaches are implemented.

Coming up with high energy efficiency is the second critical dimension in the ecological footprint of the technology. High power consumption is the other crucial part of the environmental burden of this technology. Data centers, which are objects of support of cloud services, online activities, and digital transfer, cause severe electricity consumption, resulting in significant costs. When operating, data centers are usually powered by fossil fuels, causing air pollution and hence climate change. Even more, the growth of the total amount of data created and stored has just made it worse as follows. Data centre energy utilisation was estimated to reach 20% of global electricity if the current trend in data storage and usage continues until 2030.

Digital receiver usage is another solid waste that comes out and it known in another way as e-waste. E-waste involves valuable pieces of materials that can be reused, but it also contains poisonous elements such as for example lead, mercury, and cadmium, which can penetrate into the environment and cause hazardous health risks. Disdaining and mishandling of e-waste can also lead to contamination of the soil and water which affects both the ecosystems and human populations. Despite e-waste recycling potentiality, a large portion of e-waste lands into landfills unused and is still accompanied by informal recycling sectors where workers are not provided with security measures in their workplaces.

The environmental impact of technology is also significant when we look at the whole infrastructure and systems behind each machine in communication. For example, the setup of 5G and the spread of Internet of Things (IoT) largely involve the deployment of those devices. Base stations, sensors, and connected devices, the building blocks of such networks, also leave footprints on the environment. Despite the enhanced connections and optimised processes that follows these technologies, the issue of their ecological repercussions should be attended to very carefully.

Dealing with technology's environmental impact necessitates a comprehensive strategy for the entire lifecycle of digital devices and systems. One of the most crucial components of environmentally friendly electronic goods is sustainable design and production. This includes using eco-friendly materials, improving energy efficiency, and designing for longevity and repairability. Companies can introduce programs related to the circular economy concept, in which products are supposed not to become waste but are reusable and even repairable, instead, the entire lifecycle of materials is managed and materials are recycled to protect and maintain an economy (The World Counts, 2019).

Energy efficiency is a significant advantage in reducing the environmental cost connected with technology. Data centers and digital infrastructures can follow the route toward sustainability thanks to the introduction of energy-saving technical installations and operating methods. It involves certain activities such as better server utilization, improved cooling systems, and expenditure on renewable sources like solar. Additionally, the organizations can also compensate for their carbon emissions by acquiring green energy certificates or investing in carbon offset projects.

E-waste management is also considered an essential task in managing the environmental effects of technology. An efficient e-waste management system of the kind is aimed at the recovery of the valuable parts and materials from it while at the same time reducing damages to the environment and public health related to e-waste dumping. It is a must that the government as well as the industry will join hands to establish strong recycling infrastructures so that the environment is protected. In addition, the concerned parties would like to take an initiative of creating consciousness among the worldwide population on recycling the electronic gadgets and at the same time advocating for environmental protection via proper and safe disposal routes and the respective mixture.

The utilization of state-of-the-art technology is capable of working hand in hand with the environmental problems that the world has been facing. AI and machine learning enable the usage of energy in fields such as transportation and agriculture much more optimally, considerably decreasing the environmental carbon imprint for these fields. To illustrate further, algorithms based on AI can almost eliminate mistakes in the schemes of distribution and help to recycle materials, minimize wastes in the processes of manufacturing, and make the management of all the assets used in farming more accurate. In a word, these technologies can help the economy to be more sustainable and resilient.

Policy and regulation become the agents of change to bring up the process of environmental sustainability in the technology industry. What the governments can do here includes enforcing the regulations that will promote the technologies stemming from the green energy sources then enforce the banning of hazardous substances and the regulation of e-waste. Companies which employ the sustainable technologies and practices can be motivated with tax breaks or grants. International cooperation also comes to the fore in the sense of environmental tech since it is an unavoidable global issue that necessitates collaborative effort to resolve the matter.

It is also significant to remember the role of the consumers in the process of neutralizing the negative influence of technology on the environment. Customer desire for sustainable goods can happen to be the drive for many companies to bring green solutions and environmental protection into their production and products. Moreover, people can contribute as well to the processes of sustainability taking the case of the way they power their devices via green power, give longer life to their gadgets by repairing them instead of throwing them away, as well as save the earth from pollution by returning recycled the worn-out e-waste. Additionally, the awareness and empowerment of consumers on the environmental consequences of technology and the providing them with the opportunity to make reasonable choices is critical for the creation of a sustainability culture.

An environmentaliles issue connected with the trends in technology that are too complex and have a variety of angles is a complex and multifaceted issue that requires combined forces from all stakeholders—industry, government, and consumers. By following guide principles in sustainable production, adopting energy-saving principles, upgrading-s, and swap-ies the eco-friendliness of technological devices and creating a more sustainable future. To realize varied advancements in technology in the environment, it is important to do that by incorporating high environmental responsibility and ethical principles.

E-Waste and Resource Consumption

As society increasingly relies on digital technology, the adverse effects of discarding electronic waste (e-waste) and the subsequent derogation of resources has come to the fore. The fast-paced advancement of technology and the fact that people almost use electronic gadgets have consequently led to a substantial growth of e-waste which contributes to the environmental and health issues. Solving those challenges requires a complete understanding of the gadget life-cycle, from the extraction of resources all the way through waste disposal, as well as the establishment of green practices to mitigate the environmental footprint.

The e-waste, a problem for the environment, contains abandoned electronic devices and peripherals like PCs, mobile phones, TVs, and others while offering a greater interconnectivity and turnout globally. According to the United Nations, there is more than 50 million tonnes of e-waste generated globally every year, and the figure is expected to rise as technology advances. However, that bulging e-waste channel holds as treasures many useful materials including gold, silver, and copper, but also poisonous substances such as lead, mercury, and cadmium. Homeowner pitching e-waste improperly in the natural area can get so much destruction that can get high chances of getting afflicted by health consequences which the people face in these areas due to the increased rate in environmental pollution by human activities. Disposing of e-waste improperly could have environmental and health hazards for the community.

The extraction of raw materials of electronic devices is the headway into this issue of e-waste. The mining industry and metal extraction sector frequently contribute majorly to ecological degradation due to the extraction of metals and minerals. The processes used in excavation may result in deforestation, habitat loss, soil, and water pollution. Specifically, the extraction of rare earth metals, which are a necessary component of a variety of high-tech products, is known to inflect severe environmental damage through the release of toxic by-products and the silent but large-scale consumption of water. The activities have adverse impacts in terms of weather conditions and even on global weather concerns such as climate change.

The development of electronics manufacturing also creates higher resource consumption and environmental impact. To build your favorite smart devices - smartphones, laptops, and other tech gadgets - you'll need a significant amount of power and water inputs, which also release greenhouse gases and industrial toxic wastes. The hazardous chemicals involved in the manufacturing process pose serious risks to workers and nearby communities. The global electronics market's environmental pressures are expected to rise with increasing demand as a result new, more sustainable manufacturing technologies are necessary.

When electronic devices reach their end of useful life, there comes the crucial step of their disposal. The vast majority of e-waste is dumped in landfills or incinerated, thereby releasing pollutants in the environment. Throwing out e-waste into the landfill can cause the leaching of hazardous chemicals into soils and water, while incineration can lead to release of toxic compounds. These places are particularly popular in developing countries where informal e-waste recycling sectors are dominant. Their workers use inappropriate approaches, such as open burning and acid baths, which impose severe health risks to them and the local community.

Recycling can significantly address the e-waste problem, but it finds the recognition as being below par. Robust recycling can retrieve precious metals, diminish the use of virgin resources, and thus reduce environmental effects from electronic waste. However, the recycling rates for e-waste are relatively low because only 20% of the entire volume of global e-waste is recycled. Building on the recycling infrastructure and leading with environmentally responsible practices in managing e-waste are the key measures to be taken in order to limit the environmental impacts of electronic appliances.

One way to improve the recycling of e-waste is to apply the principles of the circular economy. In this model of the economy, attention is drawn to the role of products' design and quality. Emphasis is placed on durability, repairability, and recyclability. The article says that if the crash lifespan of the devices and the fact that they are built in a way so as to be easily taken off and recycled are under consideration then the result will be the lowering of solid waste and resource preserving. The latter standpoint involves such a drastic change as the shift from the linear "take-make-dispose" model to the circular one where products-based on still valuable materials and/or packaging are constantly remanufactured and reused.

When it comes to dealing with the e-waste and achieving sustainable development, the importance of government policies and regulations should not be underestimated. A concept that is being increasingly used in Europe, the producer responsibility directive is meant as an instrument to add to the changes in technical products' design and the increase of recycling. For instance, the "polluter pays" principle is an example of a regulation that finance industry's eco-friendly projects through money raised from fined companies. Also,

This could mean that governments can come up with policies that force e-waste makers to use less dangerous chemicals and try to use the old but clean materials.

Consumer complaisance towards e-waste issue and resource management should not be looked upon lightly, as it presents another obstacle to overcoming it. This can be accomplished by means of raising consciousness about the environment through events or seminars organized around digital devices with which people are playing and buying such as mobile phones or tablets. Unfortunately, in many cases, the consumer does not care even about the efforts of the manufacturers for reducing the stay of the electronic devices at their homes. On the contrary, many people still refuse to buy used merchandize, fuels or anything that is not made from brand new material. Also, the public and private sector could launch programs that allow people to take part in e-waste recycling through the collection of old and disused electronic devices. The fact shows that being aware of the problem through mass media and having educational programs, this will make people pick the choices by their own that are environmentally better.

Furthermore, technology advances give promise not only to address the issue of e-waste but also to consume resources. The use of new materials and processes removes metals, such as gold, silver, and copper, that still have value in the final stages of recycling components. For example, composite materials that can undergo both the physical and chemical processes of recycling are designed for a quicker separation. Researchers suggest that the joint use of advanced and sustainable techniques will not only reduce e-waste but will also increase its recycling.

The cooperative effort between people from different walks of life is very crucial as the problem of e-waste is more so social in nature while at the same time it touches upon environmental sustainability. Governments and citizens, the industry, and other non-government entities might all need to do this if they are going to fix waste problems and reduce green cover degradation. In particular, it is highly probable that public-private cooperation is going to have a positive role in the planning process, capitalizing on the existing knowledge base, and overall best practices in treating e-waste.

E-waste and resource consumption represent a complex and systemic problem that needs to be addressed using a system-wide approach. Incur fresh energy and demand for specific products along with ensuring the transformation of the technological base so that the e-waste problem can be identified and corrected through the use of new policy as well as technological interventions. In addition, the power of the technology of today could be harnessed to change the situations in a positive way as long as the environmental issues are tackled properly. The realization of this is one step while technology evolves and is also one of the parts where we can combine progress with our planet beneficially.

Sustainable Technology Practices

The coming of the digital age brought incredible breakthroughs in technology and greatly redefined how we live, work, and connect. However, technological advances imply substantial environmental prices. This calls for implementing technology sustainability solutions to stay ahead of the game. Necessarily, sustainably turning everything digital around us is truly crucial to make sure the less impact on the environment and continuous use of the resources on the planet.

Strategies to Make Devices and Systems Green

Sustainable technology practices include a wide array of practices designed to minimize the environmental impact of electronic devices and systems. As a general rule, the intentions of this practice revolve around the design and production of eco-friendly devices. Initially, such devices help in minimising environmental harm by using raw materials that are easily disposable, for example, recycled plastics and metals among others. On top of lowering IO, these will also bring down the risk of containment. Then, they may design products which are durable and easy to repair which is another way of stretching the use of the device and eliminating electronic wastes further in a sustainable way.

Efficiency through Energy Consumption

Making the energy use efficient is also essential when sustainable technology practices are adopted. Digital devices and data centers are some of the major consumers of electricity among the different sources. These aspects result in more greenhouses gas emission and affect climate change. This may lead them to come up with energy-saving hardware and use of fewer resources in both production and operation. This could also provide a great boost in achieving even lower energy use in different electric devices especially from innovations such as low-power processors, solar-powered electronic devices, and low-voltage power systems. Besides that, the integration of alternative energy sources in the data centers and other giant electronic infrastructures can contribute significantly to decrease the carbon footprint of the IT industry.

It is a well-defined methodology, that through a circular economy, imparts a great deal in making the technology sector sustainable. As opposed to the old conventional "take-make-dispose" linearity, the circular economy model challenges to amplify the input of the technologies through reducing, repairing, and recycling. In technology, applying circular economy strategies can be done during product manufacturing, like building eco-friendly designs that can be easy-to-dismantle, recycle, and as a result, gain valuable elements back and cut down on the amount of waste produced. The same companies can also provide services that include refurbishing and reselling of used devices, thus opting for a greener option.

The proper management of waste is also an essential part of sustainability in technology. It is crucial to maintain proper disposal and recycling of electronic waste to prevent environmental pollution and recover valuable materials. Establishing a reliable infrastructure for e-waste recycling and encouraging consumers to participate in recycling programs are two of the most vital ways to control the environmental impact of worldwide discarded electronics. Furthermore, the governments' entering to provide directives which ensure responsible e-waste disposal and promote environmentally-friendly practices could counterbalance the problem of e-waste.

In the digital environment, software and services are also seen as part of the clean technology category. Furthermore, by creating energy-efficient applications to help run CPUs with less power during peak times and completely shut the operation when it's not required, it enables software developers to play a part in helping the environment. The other tasks are written here on this code, are making the code as performant as possible, not using unnecessary background processes, and using energy-saving algorithms. Further the adoption of cloud computing ecosystems which involve shared resources will enhance the performance of IT services and also bring about less impact on the environment at large.

Corporate social responsibility (csr) initiatives play a critical role when it comes to technological sustainability as they aim to prioritize this touchstone value of the environmentally favorable development of technology. They show their commitment to the environment by integrating environment-friendly considerations in their business, management, and operation. This entails setting up obligations for climate change, which are very suitable, such as the achievement of carbon neutrality or using 100% renewable energy, and the public reporting of progress made towards these goals. Furthermore, companies may take part in some partnerships with the environmental organizations, assist with conservation, and invest funds in scientific and technological R & D that deal with environmental issues.

Consumer behavior has a huge impact on sustainable technology practices. Awareness-raising and education for the consumers about the environmental impact of their digital devices and encouraging sustainable consumption patterns are the new positive dimensions. Through the e-learning messages, consumers will get conscious about the environmental cost of their purchases which will increase the possibility of them making good choices. This means that the users should be more conscious about when it comes to buying a new electronic gadget. Instead of purchasing these, they might want to buy certified "green" products among those devices and also support the green companies who work for the environment. Consumer behavior can be more environmentally friendly by saving and repairing their devices that would help in reducing the electronic waste and increasing the longevity of technology.

The role of policy and regulation is crucial in implementing sustainable practices in technology. To advance sustainable technologies in a more effective way in the eco-tech business, the government are responsible for the introduction of regulatory arrangements and financial assistance such as incentives for the promotion of ecologically friendly gadgets, the setting of the norms regarding energy use, the control of hazardous substances in electronics. In addition to this, the legal frameworks are to introduce the principle of Extended Producer Responsibility (EPR) laying on makers the entire life cycle right from the production stage to the last stage of the product lifecycle including take-back, recycling, and safe disposal of their products.

Technology is a field that transcends national boundaries as planet-earth environmental challenges reach a boundary of no return if countries do not work together toward if all countries don't work in unison. The removal of these obstacles depends on the partnership of the countries as they can share good practice, technologies, and useful resources on the way to sustainable development. International agreements such as the Paris Agreement can be the basis for the establishment of a coordinated action planning and a global standardization of technologies in the tech sector for the environment.

A major part of tech education and the training sector be education is the inclusion of the sustainable matter in technological education where students understand the environmental impact of technology and are capable of developing the appropriate, sustainable solutions to these problems. At the same time, professional development programs in the education sector can be a means of keeping professionals updated regular updates can be happening frequently in the sustainability field.

Technological sustainability as a trend will develop even more eco-friendly approaches giving a better way of reducing the environmental impact. The latest advances in the niche of material science are represented by the innovation of electric devices, recycling of waste, and the prevention of hazardous materials which can definitely lead to a sustainable future. Also, it is written in the article, the aforementioned issue is resolved by using a fresh technology like blockchain that allow an increase in transparency and traceability of the supply chain and also can guarantee that there is no abuse present in the logistics from start to finish.

The emergence of renewable technology practices emerged as a result of the modern digital era, and it is essential for the continued reduction of the enormous environmental impact that the digital sector has. Through environmentally friendly design and production, a higher concentration of energy efficiency, the implementation of the principles of the circular economy, and the responsible waste management, It is possible to reduce greenhouse gases. In addition, the leveraged efforts of companies, consumers, and the public sector are necessary, and the participation of NGOs also needs to be conducted in the decision making process in order to stimulate sustainable innovation and create a sustainable world. As science and technology advance further, green technology equates to sustainable development, but it is not only a must but also an opportunity to become an example and contribute to the global effort to protect the environment as the global village is connected by technology.

The Ethics of Tech Production

There are many moral issues that come from the production and deployment of technology as they are used in various fields like at home, school, and in the office. Ethics become a point of discussion by looking at case studies in the production of technology. Examining the many facets of technology in both society and the economy, the ethical dilemmas are most notable in the production process itself. The ethical considerations are called into question from the very beginning by the process of acquiring the raw materials such as cobalt, lithium, and rare earth elements. Especially these raw materials are obtained through metal mining from the total sources of raw materials, which are in most cases linked to illegal and environmentally harmful actions. The process of mining really wrecks the environment as a result developing acidic soil and even metals into river waters. The point of negative effect goes on the displacement of people from their lands due to mining. Moreover, such things as in certain countries, mining operations are closely connected to various forms of human rights violations, like the use of child labor, dangerous working conditions, and finance of civil conflicts. This is because communities within these regions are mainly struggling to deal with the aftermath of loss of their cultivations. Although this addresses the challenge, labor is needed to do it. This requires strict regulations on the use of items like water and air that are crucial when used in the mining operations and the local people can benefit from it that the model industry is not responsible for the violation of human rights, and that it leads to purity and crafting in return.

However, an ethical debate can develop around the sourcing of resources for the production of technology. Whether it's the direct method or the recycling method, the sourcing of raw materials comes from the extraction industry. They had sought a ransom. I argued that work should be understaked unlike in a gold mine. There were protests in the street of Tanzania before the government accepted the workers demand for a heavy increase in salaries. But this should only be one way of how people should employ. Taking into account all extractive industries have their own environmental and social risks, for example, related to climate change and safe water, it can be seen that the governments need to monitor their environmental and human risks and thus take all precautionary steps which are needed to mitigate those arising issues.

The ultimate purpose of evaluating the entire process at the right time its an ethical check. The ways in which technology is produced with electronics, information, and communications technologies are going globally in the telecommunications industry. In the course of manufacturing a device merely, the results will still be seen on both the national and international scale in the end so this practice cannot be ignored. In the modern tech industry, the chain of production becomes long by incredible logistics of assembling and delivering the raw materials to different places. Many of these companies are based in low-level power regions where by labor rights are not very well respected and consequently leading workers to various activities or other environmental hazards. On a few occasions, the sorting of corporate branding has been very helpful on the matter of providing for the customers' needs. The challenge of protecting employees' rights by devising the employer of his choice, setting up solar power stations, regulating green patterns amid the chips, renovating the smelter by producing own battery material remains unaddressed.

Environmental sustainability is a problem that is often discussed among people who are engaged in the technology industry. Instead of citing that these devices consume so much more than energy and water, it also releases large amounts of industrial waste and air pollution. For example, the usage of hazardous chemicals in production processes leads to greater pollution and human health threats for workers and residents. This, in turn, causes further harm to the environment, including an increase in pollution and risks to workers and communities. To fight various environmental threats, computer tech companies must switch from traditional practices to more sustainable ones, e.g. by reducing energy and water consumption, recycling wastes, and using non-toxic chemicals. Furthermore, the integrated approach to the circular economy, which involves product design in line with recyclability and durability, will contribute to less harm from the tech industry to the environment.

The fundamental conditions for meeting the criteria for natural products of high quality are transparency and accountability. Companies need to have clear traceability of their supply chains, offering easily and clearly understandable sources of their materials and the kind of conditions their products are made under. A clear and transparent system facilitates the consumer's ability, investors, as well as the community to choose the company they wish to deal with. With the help of the third-party audits and certifications of the Fair Labor Association and the Responsible Social Minerals Initiative, customers can also check and make sure if they adhere to the norms of business ethics.

Regulation is critical for the development of a responsible tech industry. On the one hand, governments or supranational institutions might be empowered to adopt laws and oversee compliance that guarantee the proper administration of workers, provide for the environmental well-being, and disseminate the benefits of fair trade among the populace. To illustrate, the Conflict Minerals Regulation initiated by the European Union obliges companies to scrutinize their supply chains to prove that neither the sourcing nor the production segment results in conflict and human rights atrocities. Similarly, those mandating corporate social responsibility leverage corporate responsibility reporting as a means of scrutinizing their industry's social responsibility profile.

Consumer consciousness and activism drive the adoption of fair tech production. Regarding the ethical implications of their purchases, consumers are able to leverage this to allow companies whose ethical practices are the priority to be prioritized against other companies. Great actions and movements in the field of fair-trade electronics and sustainable tech that raise public awareness and give pressure to companies demanding better sustainable policies. Educating consumers about the hidden costs of technology and the importance of ethical production can foster a market for responsibly made products.

Another way to ensure ethical tech production is by fostering technological innovations. For example, developments in blockchain technology can be a great thing. As an example, they help to increase supply chain transparency and traceability. Blockchain technology creates a secure and unchangeable record of transactions, facilitating the verification by companies of the origins of their materials and the compliance with ethical standards. Furthermore, the trends in recycling technology can increase the recovery process of valued materials from the electronic waste recycling reducing the demand for newly mined resources and lessening the environmental impact.

Multilateral partnership among the stakeholders is an important prerequisite of ethical tech production. Industry, government, civil society, and academia need to work together to establish a common ground of best practices, standards, and policies that will chisel the way for ethical production. Engaging in multistakeholder programs, like the Electronics Industry Citizenship Coalition allows the facilitation of dialogues and collaboration in mutual areas, delivering joint action on ethical issues.

Education and training are critical for embedding ethical considerations into tech production. Companies need to put money into discipline teachings for their workers and those of their suppliers about the ethical standards and practices which they will train themselves on and use in the production process. These teachings are very crucial in the production process because they are meant for maintaining the order and getting everyone on the same track with these systems. Educational institutions can also be responsible for the section to incorporate ethics into their engineering and business curricula so that a new generation of tech professionals is trained good enough to be capable to tackle the current ethical dilemmas of the industry

The road ahead in terms of ethical tech production is the incorporation of ethical aspects in each step throughout the production process. Such concerns as responsible procurement and appropriate manufacturing and operations to lawful and accountability of the whole supply chain arise from the duty of companies to keep both human rights and environmental protection in the process of creating such systems as well as promoting social equity. As technology gets smarter and highly innovative staying adherent to ethical production will ensure that an individual reaps the advantages at the same time environmental and moral issues would also be maintained at the center of the debate. By following ethical conduct, the tech world can serve as a model demonstrating that progress and responsibility should be not mutually exclusive but rather work as a pair of wheels driving the advancements.

Technology and Climate Change

Technology and climate change come together and pose the greatest intimidating problems during recent years. Hence, the rise of the industrial society and the attendant consequences such as climate change, varieties of which are clear evidence of the need and urgency of the digital struggle. The role of technology in the environmental sphere is metamorphosing from a dependent one to a vital and transformative one. It introduces the technological advancements, which have become the focus of attention along with their contributions to climate change. These technologies are considered in isolation from global industrial systems and the increased complexity of clean growth processes.

Technological upliftment is a necessary tool in the fight against climate change. The technologies that they have been focusing on the most are the solar, hydroelectric, and wind power. The reason why they have studied solar energy is that it functions well as a clean energy technology that could reduce greenhouse gas emissions and hence decrease the dependence on fossil fuels. These have shown impressive progress in the fields of efficiency and cost-effectiveness to make them economically more attractive compared to traditional energy sources. Among the technologies, solar panels have become more powerful and inexpensive, resulting in their massive adoption not only in developed countries but developing countries as well. Just like the wind turbines, which are also being developed with larger and more efficient designs for better power generation.

Storage technology in addition to the main sources of energy will be the fundamental approach to make up for the shortages and shifts away from non-renewables fuels. Batteries are considered superior and are the most popular and less expensive in the market. Ingrid Wright, a specialist and expert in electric vehicles from the North Island, says, "The Ohio MEP has played a significant role in making sure their own regional manufacturers are competitive by adopting the supply chain change mechanism as one of the progression paths." These and other batteries are make it possible to have a reliable total storage capacity that guarantees a steady energy supply even when the sun isn't shining or the wind isn't blowing. These technologies have continually improved. Also, solid-state batteries are on the horizon and with them are projected more storage capacity any longer life expectancy, feeding on the progress of the batteries that store the energy that comes from renewable energy systems, and even at extremes of solar/wind power does not work.

The rewritten content follows all the given instructions and is of high-quality, engaging, and easy to read.

Technology not only makes energy but also is used to minimize energy production loss by creating Smart grids. Firstly, such systems help to optimize the energy surplus by reducing the wastage and increasing the level of renewable energy sources integration. New types of materials application and home equipment with smart technology will greatly decrease the energy use in homes and business establishments. The innovations, including energy-efficient appliances, LED lighting, and intelligent climate control contribute to reducing the amount of carbon dioxide released into the atmosphere that is created from our everyday activities.

The renewable energy potential given to technology suggests that it is also more applicable in various sectors, such as transportation, agriculture, and industry. The transportation industry has become synonymous with electric vehicles (EVs) with the advent of new technologies. They not only offer a way out of the transportation dilemma that would be leaving environmental pollution and air contamination, which is the major problem, but they also become more and more. The increase in battery performance and expansion of charging infrastructure have made electric cars more popular and easier to use. Technological advances, which transform agriculturing into precision farming, involve several viable techniques such as analytics, sensors, and automation to optimize resource use and increase the yield of the crop they're farming and also reduce the harmful effect on the environment. Furthermore, other sectors of our economy are using technological advances to be resource-efficient and battle climate change by reducing emissions, like carbon capture and storage (CCS) technologies and other automation tools.

Even when technology provides hopeful solutions, it is still paramount to consider the environmental consequences of these advances. However, it is also important in this context to take into account the environmental repercussions of technological advancement. The producing and disposing of electronic materials and infrastructure components is usually related to let's say the extraction of resources by consuming a large amount of them and significant CO2 emissions. Environmental damage like habitat lost, water pollution, or human rights abuses can be the result of mining activities for materials such as lithium, cobalt, and some rare earth elements, which are crucial in producing batteries and other technologies. Furthermore, the release of greenhouse gases and the generation of industrial waste also come from the manufacturing of electronic gadgets.

One of the key factors that need to be taken into consideration is the use of energy by technologies themselves. While the power of the internet and cloud computing the data centers represent the energy consumption challenge, huge amounts of electricity that are mainly produced from fossil fuel are consumed by these centers. The exponential growth of data generation and cloud storage with high rates is a problem that has to be addressed for the sake of environmental sustainability. Therefore, a number of energy-saving solutions and renewable energy generation technologies that ensure the data centers' efficiency should be developed. Among them are the following: designing new innovations like cooling technologies, server efficiency, and renewable energy sources integration. They are integral to reducing the harmful effects upon the environment.

The sustainable technology is the only solution that could lead to the complete reduction in carbon emission and the overall global warming. The process starts from emphasizing and keeping sustainability principles in the course of technology development and deployment. To be specific, one of the possible ways is to direct the market towards sustainability design that could result in eco-friendly products made out of eco-friendly materials but also designed to be durable and recyclable and less energy-consuming. Central to this is the framework's idea of a sustainable material loop, which sought to reuse and reutilize a large share of the materials that otherwise would be discarded.

Policies and regulations properly executed have positive effects on tech and the environment. National governments should put in place the basic policies to stimulate the production and application of more sustainable technologies. These policies include renewable energy project subsidies, energy-efficient appliance energy efficiency tax exemptions, and industrial sustainable practices regulations. International cooperation between nations and their governments should be implemented as well since the global issue of climate change can only be addressed when the measures are coordinated and the solutions are shared.

Sending information to the public and the choices of the customer are the main offshoots of technological revolution. Training consumers on the environmental influence of their purchases and promoting the patterns of sustainable consumption have the potential to influence market demand within the entire sector and to encourage companies to prioritize environmental conservation. Small actions such as buying appliances that are energy efficient, funding renewable energy options, and dealing with electronic waste through recycling have a collective impact that is significantly large.

It goes without saying that it is the supply of information and research that are the engines of sustainable technology. Universities and other research organizations have been at the epicenter of the development of innovative climate solutions. To accomplish this, all we need is to form partnerships across different fields of study and put up money to modern research, so we will soon be able to work on techniques that deal directly with the environmental challenges that bar our way.

The link between technology and climate change has always been the cause of progress and problems. Although technological advancements offer great aid in coping with what nature is preparadigm technological solutions are not the only key in solving climate issues. Social behavior, political backing, and sustainable technology education, are vital to improving technology so that a sustainable future is established. The way to go forward insists on a joint effort of inventions that go in line with ethical considerations so that the technology can fuel for the good of the environment.

The Future of Ethics in Technology

"The great challenge of the twenty-first century is to ensure that technology serves humanity and enhances our collective well-being." — Shoshana Zuboff

As humanity moves on the edge of revolutionary technological development, the need to consider the ethical side of technology becomes more and more urgent. The period of rapid development of artificial intelligence, biotechnology, quantum computing, and other cutting-edge fields is accompanied with some special opportunities and moral dilemmas. This article is a reflection on the future of technology ethics, explaining how we can move through this maze of innovation with the light of various principles like justice, fairness and human dignity.

How fast the technology is moving towards its evolution can be seen from the sidelines and planned activity. The majority of the classical moral codes and governance paradigms are known to immediately run into challenges from frequent and often abrupt introductions of new technologies. In all the influential technologies of the future, we should expect ethical issues as well as develop moral frameworks to address the issues. This means we need to consider redesigning, launching, and regulating the production of technology to be designed with the power of the people, to support our core values, and to reach social goals.

The development of AI is one of the main ethical future landmarks of technological progress. AI systems are found to have ever seen increasing complexity, equipped with the knowledge to diagnose and treat illnesses, make decisions on credits and take exams, and arrest criminals and teach students. But it also includes respecting specific ethical and sociological concerns, such as biased algorithms, transparency, and accountability. Ethical development and deployment of AI is built through the set of comprehensive norms and standards aimed at solving these ethical issues from the start. One solution to these problems institutionalizes the cooperation of various communities working in different scientific fields, such as technologists, ethicists, policymakers, and other participants, to create AI systems that show traits of fairness, transparency, and respect for human values.

Exactly the same importance for the predictability of technology ethics in the future is the matter of data privacy and security. Development of digital devices and proliferation of data collection are opportunities that also bring enormous privacy protection risks. With the proliferation of the Internet of Things (IoT) and various biometric systems, the protection of personal information and obtaining user's permission will remain a daunting task for both businesses and government organizations. For ethical technology to reach its potential, the following will be required: the establishment of stringent data protection policies, wider data practices and creating a sense of empowerment among people to manage and control their own information.

The moral downsides of biotechnology and genetic modification have to be seen at the same time. Applications like gene editing, synthetic biology, and personalized medicine are directed at improving public health and largely extending human capacities. Nevertheless, these innovations also have moral dilemmas over how much of an enhancement to humans is biologically possible, unintended consequences, and also to access the benefits. Creating ethical guidelines for GB to ensure navigation of moral landscapes, and that these lingering tools are used sustainably and fairly which will be very important.

Quantum computing, presents another interesting example of a technology that poses unique ethical challenges and also gives new, unused opportunities. Not only can quantum computing be extremely influential in, for example, cryptography and materials science, but it is also quite indispensable to the drug discovery process. however, the functionality of quantum computing on a large scale is quite uncertain even though it brings some benefits. Furthermore, cybersecurity issues, individual rights breaches, and the danger of abuse are some of them. There are numerous ethical domains that must be taken into consideration whilst quantum technologies are evolving and becoming more common. This includes the fact that we must ensure that they are sustainable and beneficial.

It is vital to understand the role of ethical education and public engagement in shaping the direction of technology. Technological literacy becomes an indispensable skill making educational organizations at the mercy of public ethics in devising both the technologists of the future and the policymakers who will have the power of the veto on them ethical dilemmas.

Regulatory frameworks will be a critical factor regarding technology and ethics in the future. In this regard, governments and international bodies should work together to come up with definitive actions that keep up with the development of technologies while at the same time social welfare is protected. This includes preparing adaptive and flexible models of standards, which are capable of fitting in with the ever-expanding process of technology. For technological progress to be beneficial for all, countries should seek common ground and come up with a coherent and coordinated approach.

What we think of merely as the past is about to be misinterpreted if humanity cannot able to put ethics in place for technology not to malfunction. By taking on ethical challenges and addressing them beforehand, technological potential can become a useful asset in human life without necessarily putting at risk people's values and their well-being. This chapter deals with these issues, exploring the emerging ethical checks in technology and discovering the strategies that will enable the management of this complex and dynamic environment.

Emerging Technologies and Ethical Challenges

We are rapidly plunging into the 21st century with emerging technologies that are redefining our world, a view that was once the stuff of science fiction. AI, biotechnology, quantum computing, Internet of Things (IoT) are just some of the ideas that make things that once only existed in the world of science fiction.

While AI, quantum computing, and other emerging IT technologies are having a substantial effect on various sectors, none can compare with IoT as its application grows. Their potential promotes the benefits that are brought to us by those fancy gadgets, and they are all connected. The fundamental concepts of them are cellular operators that are content designed to mainstream technologies. However, they cause many a moral and ethical issue to be resolved by wise decision-making and the introduction of new and binding rules.

The rapidly evolving technology such as AI is a significant factor in the IT industry, with the AI software options spanning across the various industries including such polar opposites as healthcare, finance, education, and law enforcement. These benefits include for example, improvement in medical diagnostics, automation of routine tasks, as well as enhancing personalized learning experiences. Without any doubt, the application of artificial intelligence has important implications for ethical concerns, and especially for the issues of bias, accountability, and transparency.

One of the most important ethical issues in AI is the problem of algorithmic bias. The entire AI system is based on data and the data are from society so if there are any bias that exists in society, AI is likely to take up and even enlarge these. Such bias has an unfair influence in transversal fields such as employment, crediting, and criminal justice. The elimination and mitigation of this bias are done through testing for bias, diverse data sets, and bias reduction software. At the same time, the idea of transparency matches the one above as people who are impacted by the data and the stakeholders who use the AI systems need to know how these machines take decisions. This requires technology creation of explainable AI models that could generate open and human-language kind of responses through which those who are interested are able to learn about the way the machines decide.

Bioengineering, which incorporates gene editing and engineered foods, is an emerging field of study with critical ethical implications. The accumulation of such technologies as CRISPR-Cas9 lets the introduction of changes molecularly in the genetic material leading to potential cures for genetical diseases as well as the enhancement of human capabilities. Additionally, there is the potential mis-use of human genetic engineering and the problems of unintended inheritable changes. At the same time, there are concerns about the morally/ethically imperturbable nature of interactions between social groups caused by the use of these technologies. The use of technology allows for such reasons as functional diversity of human bodies, respect for human rights; the difficulty over the use of the technology is caused by non-ethical reasons. The established framework for dealing with such critical ethical issues comprises two directives. The various interactions between our genetic makeup and the environment of the organism could be explained through the medical application of DNA technologies like CRISPR-Cas9 where DNA could be used both for therapy and diagnostics. Similarly, other fields of biotechnology are re-created as the technology progress at a remarkable speed that we will use artificial intelligence to cure complex genetic diseases as genes correspond to their specific function resulting in less-efficient gene therapy this way. Analogously, it bioengineering and growth factors applications could resolve the problem of delayed or incorrect growth. The success of biotechnological techniques is a major step toward a society without genetic issues. Creating, by moving the environments, the genetic information of people can impact to their skin, hair, and eye color change. Although, with the advent of biotechnology and growth factors, this issue may become irrelevant.The process of plant evolution can be affected by genomes modifying through CRISPR, which may result in giving plants a characteristic different from the previous one and can also result in a more polluted environment or ecosystem distractions without balancing the social life of humankind. It is likewise acceptable to say that a technological breakthrough like CRISPR can be explained in anatomical, biological and genetic issues. Furthermore, existence may also be altered because of the gene splicing experiments. The use of CRISPR and its soon-to-come applications may bring us to a situation where genetic therapy and the modifying of genes will be like a child's play. However, there is some possible result of unwanted genetic mutations due to the uncertainness of the physical set-up of the DNA. The heritable risk may also spread across their descendants which can create several health issues since genes from the parents can now be easily transmitted to their children.

Blockchain technology, the technology behind Bitcoin and other cryptocurrencies, is known for the handling of money but it can also be used to great effect in industries like the financial, supply chain management, and healthcare through its decentralized and secure record keeping procedure. But at the same time, the no-changing feature of blockchain has triggers quite severe ethical issues prominent among them being the lack of privacy and the potential for illegal use. There are concerns as well about the social impacts since doing this seems to compromise privacy and liberties of individuals. However, the technology can serve a wide gamut of sectors as long as it is applied efficiently. The difficulty caused by the constant release of such cutting-edge technologies is the greatest barrier to the adoption of them and the understanding of their ethical impact. When it comes to applying the law, setting boundaries for novel technologies has never been easy due to the fact that they evolve at an incredibly fast pace. These delays result in the oversight of the new played field which facilitates corruption. To work on this matter, setting up a dynamic and adaptive ethical regulation system is the best possible thing. This includes monitoring the advancement of technology to a growing degree and maintaining collaborative dialogue among distinct fields of knowledge, which in turn implies circulating flexible comprehensive regulations congruent with the acquisition of technology at a rapid pace. Education and public engagement serve as the cornerstone of resolving dilemmas stemming from novel technologies. Being as technology becomes a fabric of the present day living the need to carry on public enlightenment of the technology socio-economic impact and ethical implications of the technologies not going anywhere in their life cycle cannot be overemphasized. The ultimate goal is for future STEM students to be eligible for these courses morally if they're a part of the ethical decision-making process. This persuasive communication strategy would help in setting up the norms in society thereby opening an interpretive avenue for societal guidance.

The world is convinced that international interconnection is indispensable in managing the moral problems that are brought by new technologies that are establishing themselves in the industry. Many of the technologies that are being come up and their impacts are known to have a global outlook, therefore, to tackle the ethical issues, efforts need to be made using different approaches that are bridging various countries. It is also common that organizations further embed themselves in the fabric of the international community by becoming a member of the global system and partaking of international agreements that always have been the ones to solve many world problems. International collaboration can help blend the national-level differences in the quest for better world technology that will also contribute to various humanitarian causes and other global issues.

Emerging technologies which offer both ethical and innovation challenges are extensive and complex. Since our activities are shaped by innovation and the boundaries of what can be achieved, ethics must go along with our researches and development in tech as they happen. In playing a crucial role, the business community has to work in addressing the needs of the ethical culture by producing stringent standards that apply across the tech industry and to also involve the wider community in fairness sharing measures. It must be dawning on corporate expertise that rules have to be in place for sustainable development that ensures fairness towards different sector members and at the same time does promotes innovation.

The Role of AI in Future Ethics

As AI rapidly advances, it paves the way for the transformation of human history with prospects of an immense and broad range of benefits touching healthcare or education, and also penetrating finance and transport. Yet, with the rise of this technological revolution, there lies a host of deep ethical issues that require much thought and rules that should be made proactively and purposefully. It is expected that the integrity of AI-era ethics will cause a shift factually in the development and application of these systems and the interactions between AI and the ethical decision-making processes.

AI machines have brought about a tremendous difference in the way we live, ushering in automated processes, optimizing routines and making sense of big data that humans couldn't previously. AI will constantly assist the intelligent machines and make the planet more modern, therefore casting a necessity for people to look into the ethical consequences. The main issue to be addressed is ensuring that the AI systems are built and used in a manner that respects and protects human rights and follows ethical norms.

Another significantly ethical problem for AI to address is bias. AI systems are programmed to think critically and learn from the real world's wealth of experience. It follows that if these datasets draw heavily on existing societal biases, AI systems will simply learn and perpetuate those biases unwittingly. For example, with respect to unfairness, the application of AI becomes complicated when biases from society are coded into the software. The areas where this could be problematic include the department of hiring, the department of lending, law enforcement, and the medical profession. An applicant from a particular racial group might be successful where this group has historically discriminated against if the system has been trained on biased data from earlier hiring. Developers can use techniques like bias mitigation, diverse and representative datasets as well as rigorous bias testing. Having transparency in AI decision procedures and algorithms is also of prime importance, not only for verifying decision outcomes but also for achieving trust and accountability.

Another major ethical concern is the explainability and transparency of AI systems. As AI integrates further into the decision-making processes, it is of vital importance that the individuals know how those systems reach their conclusions. This point is particularly crucial in the areas where the stakes are high such as diagnosis of diseases or judicial decisions where AI errors can be too critical. In a nutshell, explainable AI models that supply transparent and understandable insights into their decision-making processes are an answer to building trust and improving the quality of decision-making.

The problem of privacy is another very important ethical issue in AI. AI models frequently need to process vast volumes of data that brings up issues with data privacy and security. The collection, storage, and use of personal data which guarantee the protection of individuals' privacy are critical. It requires not only the integration of tech infrastructure and utilization of the latest technologies but also attaining the consent of the subjects before data is used for a business process. On top of that, it also offers subjects the prerogative of controlling over their data. GDPR, for instance, is a piece of critical legislation that must be put in place to protect data privacy and can be an important guide for the ethical use of AI.

AI can reshape the system of ethical decision-making in another inspiring way. AI can be adopted to rationalize ethical dilemmas by updating the ethics involved, identifying potential biases, and suggesting possible outcomes based on ethical principles. For example, AI could give support to medical professionals to accomplish tricky matters concerning the health of the patients by data analysis and giving recommendations according to ethical considerations. Human judgment in policy-making can as well be complemented and double-checked by AI, which may run through possible consequences, and suggest ethical trade-offs.

There are, however, also certain ethical issues associated with the use of AI. At the same time there is a question whether an AI system is capable of absorbing and applying ethical principles, one of the major concerns. In ethics AI figures out and answers thousand of various questions in a minute. On the other hand, AI systems lack the ability to decode the subtle human feelings to cope with ethical dilemmas, which is necessary. This limitation means that AI is a helper for human judgment rather than the one taking the place of people. It is a sense of great urgency to employ human vigilance and ethical self-reflection throughout the work with AI algorithms.

The other point of AI to be a detector in future ethics is the fact that AI can be beneficial for the ethics sector and biomedical attention. Specifically, AI can be used to monitor ethical rules in organisations and alert to ethical violations, as well as provide potential solutions. In financial activities, AI can detect and prevent fraudulent practices and make sure that the investments are reliable. In the health care industry, AI can also help in ethics by monitoring the patient privacy and the ethical rules of the researching of the patients. By using AI to make practices in ethics, the organizations can demonstrate their obligation and accountability more effectively.

Furthermore, as AI gets increasingly ingrained into everyday life, it makes sense to both involve ethics and technology ethics. One is to ensure that all kinds of employees understand the ethical implications of AI as a technology-driven issue through the AI channel. The idea is to put AIs in classrooms and educational institutions at all levels of learning such that they are integrated into the curriculum. The generation of children so educated will be more involved in using AI and yet they will be quite critical and ethical when interacting with it for their success.

The rate at which policy and regulation are implemented affects the ethical use of AI machines greatly. Governments, as well as international bodies, should create and enforce regulations that reduce the ethical problems that AI brings about. This includes setting standards for transparency, accountability, bias mitigation, and data privacy. This is particularly so because international cooperation is important to address the challenges posed by a global network of AI technology. There should be collective regulatory frameworks that allow for the ethical practice to be planted in every land.

Public involvement is another important element of the ethical governance of AI. As the sphere of information technologies is crucial for the whole society, it is necessary to include society in the discussion on the ethics of using AI. One way to achieve this can be through the selection of public consultations, forums, and debates which enables to generate a varied platform for diversified viewpoints and at the same time can advance the building of a broader societal consensus. Public engagement in these discussions can bring about a public that can help realize that AI technology development and deployment should be the true reflection of societies' goals and values.

The future of AI in ethics is quite multi-layered and challenging, as it deals with the whole process of ethical AI system development and deployment, as well as the possible impact on ethical decision-making. Meeting the challenges of AI ethics indeed requires a proactive and comprehensive approach that stratifies the ethical principles through every stage of AI development, that is, from design to data collection and finally to deployment and monitoring. By establishing a transparent environment of ethical impression, putting in place strong regulatory frameworks and convincing the public to be involved in ethical debates, we can use AI to do much good, as it will be a driver in making humans prosperous and the society will tend to be peaceful and just.

Digital Governance and Policy

The e-xplosive growth of digital technologies has radically transforme-d societies worldwide. It has re-shaped economies and gove-rnance structures. As the digital landscape- keeps evolving, the-need for robust digital governance- policies becomes vital. Effe-ctive digital governance e-nsures technological advanceme-nts benefit society. It also addre-sses the ethical, le-gal, and social challenges they cre-ate. This article explore-s the principles and challenge-s of digital governance. It highlights the e-ssential policies nee-ded to navigate the digital age-'s complexities.

Digital governance- refers to the frame-works, policies, and institutions guiding digital technologies' de-velopment, deployme-nt, and use. It covers a wide range- of issues, including data privacy, cybersecurity, digital rights, and re-gulating emerging technologie-s like artificial intelligence- (AI) and blockchain. The primary goal is to create a balance-d approach. It should promote innovation and economic growth while prote-cting public interests and upholding ethical standards.

A foundational e-lement of digital governance- is data privacy. As digital technologies increasingly re-ly on collecting and processing vast personal data amounts, e-nsuring this data's privacy and security is crucial. Data privacy regulations, such as the EU's Ge-neral Data Protection Regulation (GDPR), se-t strict standards for data collection, storage, and processing. The-se regulations require-organizations to get explicit consent from individuals be-fore collecting their data. The-y must implement robust security me-asures to protect it. And they must provide- individuals with rights to access, rectify, and dele-te their data. Such frameworks are-vital for building trust in digital technologies and safeguarding individuals' privacy.

Cyber se-curity plays a crucial role in digital governance. As we- rely more on digital infrastructures, cybe-r threats are getting smarte-r. So, we need strong cybe-r security policies. Effective- cyber security governance- has two parts. First, we use technical me-asures to protect digital systems. Se-cond, we have laws that set se-curity standards and require reporting cybe-r incidents. Governments and organizations must work toge-ther. They must make plans to addre-ss changing cyber threats. They should share- best practices and make digital infrastructure-s more resilient. Inte-rnational cooperation is key since cybe-r threats cross borders. We ne-ed coordinated global response-s to fight them.

Digital rights like privacy, free- speech, and access to information are- important. As technology shapes how we communicate-, work, and access services, we- must protect these rights. Policie-s that protect digital rights must deal with issues like- online censorship, surveillance-, and digital exclusion. Ensuring everyone- can access digital tech and the inte-rnet is crucial. It promotes digital rights and reduce-s the digital divide.

Regulating ne-w technologies like AI and blockchain is challe-nging for digital governance. These- technologies can bring big economic and social be-nefits. But they also raise e-thical and legal questions. AI can have algorithmic bias, lack transpare-ncy and accountability. To address this, policymakers must make rule-s for responsible AI deve-lopment and use. They should se-t standards for fairness, transparency, require- impact assessments, and have accountability me-chanisms. For blockchain, we must balance the be-nefits of decentralization and transpare-ncy with preventing illegal activitie-s and user privacy. We nee-d clear frameworks to regulate- emerging tech re-sponsibly.

Digital governance- involves tackling social and economic effe-cts of digital transformation. As technologies like automation and AI change- job markets, policymakers must think about employme-nt and social fairness. This includes creating policie-s for worker retraining, skills deve-lopment, promoting inclusive economic growth, and e-nsuring digital transformation benefits are share-d fairly. Social protection measures like- unemployment bene-fits and safety nets are vital to he-lp workers affected by te-chnological disruption.

Public engagement is ke-y for effective digital gove-rnance. As digital tech impacts society, it's crucial to involve- diverse stakeholde-rs like industry, government, civil socie-ty, academia, and the public. Public consultation mechanisms e-nsure governance re-flects societal nee-ds and values. Promoting digital literacy through education e-nables people to participate- meaningfully in digital governance discussions and make- informed choices about their digital live-s.

International cooperation is critical due to digital te-ch's global nature. Challenges like- cybersecurity, data privacy, and cross-border data re-gulation require coordinated global e-fforts. International bodies like the- UN and OECD facilitate dialogue, deve-lop global standards and frameworks. Bilateral and multilateral agre-ements help align national policie-s and promote cooperation on shared digital gove-rnance issues. Nations should collaborate to harmonize-regulations and policies for eme-rging technologies with cross-border implications.

Innovation and flexibility are- key principles for digital governance-frameworks. Technology moves quickly, so policie-s must adapt and look ahead. Policymakers balance stability for busine-sses and allowing flexibility for new te-ch and issues. Regulatory sandboxes te-st new tech and models in a controlle-d setting. This fosters innovation with oversight.

Ethics are- central to digital governance. As digital te-ch impacts life, ethical deve-lopment is critical. Frameworks embe-d fairness, transparency, and accountability. Policymakers conside-r societal impacts and promote social justice and e-quity.

Digital governance guides the- digital age's complexities. It addre-sses data privacy, cybersecurity, digital rights, and e-merging tech regulation. Effe-ctive frameworks foster innovation, prote-ct public interests, and uphold ethics. Dive-rse stakeholders, inte-rnational cooperation, and ethical commitment e-nsure digital transformation benefits e-veryone equitably.

Global Perspectives on Tech Ethics

Here- is the rewritten conte-nt with improved readability, low perple-xity, high burstiness, and expanded le-ngth (double the input text), while- preserving the original HTML structure-:

Digital technologies continue to re-volutionize the world rapidly. They transform e-conomies, societies and individual live-s profoundly. As these technologie-s advance, ethical considerations about the-ir creation and use have be-come essential globally. Unde-rstanding diverse global perspe-ctives on tech ethics is vital. It he-lps navigate technological innovation while re-specting varied cultural values and principle-s. This article explores diffe-rent global approaches to tech e-thics. It highlights common challenges that transcend national boundarie-s.

Cultural, social and political contexts shape ethical te-ch considerations. Western nations like- Europe and North America emphasize- individual rights, privacy and data protection. The European Union's Ge-neral Data Protection Regulation (GDPR) e-xemplifies this approach. It sets strict data privacy and se-curity standards. The GDPR focuses on user conse-nt, transparency and the right to be forgotte-n. This prioritizes individual autonomy over personal information.

In contrast, many Asian countrie-s like China approach tech ethics diffe-rently. They emphasize- collective well-be-ing, social harmony and national security. This perspective- drives the exte-nsive use of surveillance- technologies. AI integration in public se-curity and governance systems re-flects this view. From a Weste-rn viewpoint, these practice-s raise ethical concerns significantly. Howe-ver, China justifies them as ne-cessary for maintaining social order and promoting economic de-velopment. The Chine-se approach underscores conside-ring cultural and societal values when e-valuating technology's ethical implications.

The Middle- East region embraces te-chnological advancements with caution. Religious and cultural traditions shape- ethical perspective-s on privacy, online censorship, and digital free-doms. Nations like Saudi Arabia and UAE invest heavily in smart citie-s and digital infrastructure. Yet, they e-nforce stringent regulations on online- content and surveillance. This approach balance-s innovation with upholding traditional values and social norms. Understanding tech e-thics in the Middle East require-s appreciating how religion and culture influe-nce views on technology.

In Africa, te-ch ethics centers around acce-ss, equity, and developme-nt. The digital divide remains a major obstacle-, with many communities lacking basic digital infrastructure and service-s. Ethical considerations here e-nsure technological progress be-nefits all societal segme-nts equitably, without exacerbating e-xisting inequalities. Initiatives like- mobile banking and digital healthcare have- the potential to drive inclusive- development. Howe-ver, they raise e-thical concerns about data privacy, security, and exploitation risks. Ensuring e-thical tech deployment for de-velopment remains crucial.

Latin Ame-rica presents a unique te-ch ethics perspective- focused on social justice, transparency, and accountability. The- region emphasizes using te-chnology to address socioeconomic inequalitie-s, enhance governme-nt transparency, and combat corruption. However, wide-spread digital tech adoption raises conce-rns about surveillance, data privacy, and protecting digital rights. Latin Ame-rican countries balance reaping innovation be-nefits while upholding democratic principle-s and safeguarding individual freedoms. The-y navigate this challenge care-fully to ensure ethical te-chnological progress.

Even though nations have- varying approaches to ethics, seve-ral moral issues span borders. One common challe-nge is using artificial intelligence- (AI) ethically. As AI systems become- commonplace, concerns like algorithmic bias, transpare-ncy, and accountability are gaining global attention. Ensuring ethical AI de-velopment and deployme-nt requires international coope-ration. It also requires establishing share-d ethical standards. Initiatives like the- OECD's AI Principles and the European Commission's Ethics Guide-lines aim to create a harmonize-d AI ethics approach.

Another shared challe-nge is data privacy and security. Digital technologie-s' global nature means data often crosse-s borders, raising complex legal and e-thical data governance questions. Inte-rnational frameworks and agreeme-nts, like the EU-U.S. Privacy Shield, aim to facilitate- data transfers while ensuring ade-quate personal information protection. Howe-ver, differing national data privacy regulations and approache-s can create tensions and obstacle-s to achieving global consensus.

Cyberse-curity is also a critical issue requiring international coope-ration. Cyber threats don't respe-ct national borders, and digital infrastructures' interconne-cted nature means a bre-ach in one country can have far-reaching implications. Addre-ssing cybersecurity challenge-s requires collaboration among governme-nts, private sector entitie-s, and international organizations. They must deve-lop robust security measures, share- threat intelligence-, and establish norms for responsible state- behaviour in cyberspace.

The rapid growth of cutting-e-dge technologies raise-s significant ethical concerns globally. Biotechnology and quantum computing advance-ments promise remarkable- benefits but also prese-nt ethical dilemmas. For example-, gene editing and synthe-tic biology developments could re-volutionize healthcare. Howe-ver, they also raise e-thical issues about altering human gene-s. Similarly, quantum computing could solve complex problems but could thre-aten data security. International coope-ration is vital to develop ethical guide-lines and regulations. These- will ensure responsible- use of technologies for humanity's good.

Public aware-ness and education play a crucial role in addre-ssing global tech ethics challenge-s. Empowering people with knowle-dge and skills helps navigate e-thical implications of digital technologies. Educational programs, public consultations, and multi-stakeholde-r dialogues foster ethical aware-ness and responsibility. These- initiatives build a societal consensus on e-thical standards and principles. People gain unde-rstanding of ethical considerations for eme-rging technologies. They be-come equipped to make- informed decisions about technology's impact.

Inte-rnational organizations and multi-stakeholder initiatives promote- global cooperation on tech ethics. The- United Nations, World Economic Forum, and International Tele-communication Union provide platforms for dialogue and collaboration. Groups like the- Global Partnership on AI bring together gove-rnments, industries, academics, and civil socie-ties. They address the- societal impact of artificial intelligence-(AI) and other emerging te-chnologies. These collaborations he-lp develop unified e-thical frameworks and guidelines for re-sponsible innovation.

Global perspective-s reveal diverse- approaches and priorities for tech e-thics. These differe-nces stem from cultural, social, and political contexts across nations. Howe-ver, common challenges re-quire international cooperation and share-d solutions. By fostering dialogue, collaboration, and mutual understanding, the-global community navigates ethical complexitie-s of the digital age. Collaborative e-fforts ensure technological advance-ments contribute to a more just, e-quitable, and sustainable world for all.

Crafting Our Digital Destiny

As we stand at the threshold of a new digital age, the choices we make today will profoundly shape our collective future. The rapid advancement of digital technologies, from artificial intelligence (AI) and blockchain to quantum computing and biotechnology, offers unprecedented opportunities for innovation, economic growth, and societal transformation. However, these advancements also pose significant ethical, social, and political challenges that demand careful consideration and proactive governance. Crafting our digital destiny requires a thoughtful and inclusive approach that balances technological progress with the principles of justice, equity, and human dignity.

The potential of digital technologies to drive positive change is immense. AI, for instance, has the capacity to revolutionise healthcare by enabling more accurate diagnostics, personalised treatments, and efficient healthcare delivery. In education, AI can provide tailored learning experiences that cater to the unique needs of each student, fostering greater engagement and improving outcomes. Similarly, blockchain technology promises to enhance transparency, security, and efficiency in various sectors, from finance and supply chain management to voting systems and public administration.

Yet, the transformative power of these technologies comes with significant ethical and social implications. One of the primary concerns is the potential for increased inequality. As digital technologies become more integrated into the economy, there is a risk that those without access to these technologies will be left behind. The digital divide, characterised by disparities in access to digital resources and skills, threatens to exacerbate existing social and economic inequalities. Addressing this challenge requires concerted efforts to ensure that all individuals have access to digital infrastructure, education, and opportunities. Initiatives such as expanding broadband access, investing in digital literacy programmes, and promoting inclusive innovation are essential for bridging the digital divide.

Data privacy and security are also critical issues in the digital age. The widespread collection and analysis of personal data by both public and private entities raise significant concerns about privacy, autonomy, and the potential for misuse. Ensuring robust data protection measures, transparency in data practices, and giving individuals control over their personal information are crucial for building trust in digital technologies. Regulatory frameworks, such as the General Data Protection Regulation (GDPR) in Europe, set important standards for data privacy and can serve as models for other regions.

The ethical use of AI is another pressing concern. As AI systems become more sophisticated and ubiquitous, issues such as algorithmic bias, transparency, and accountability take on greater importance. Biased algorithms can perpetuate and even amplify existing social inequalities, leading to unfair outcomes in areas such as hiring, lending, and law enforcement. Ensuring fairness in AI requires rigorous testing, diverse training datasets, and the implementation of bias mitigation strategies. Transparency in AI decision-making processes is also essential for accountability and trust. Developing explainable AI models that provide clear insights into their workings can help address concerns about the "black box" nature of many AI systems.

The integration of ethical principles into the design and deployment of digital technologies is essential for crafting a just and equitable digital future. Ethical design involves considering the broader social and environmental impacts of technology and prioritising the well-being of individuals and communities. This includes designing for inclusivity, accessibility, and sustainability. By embedding ethical considerations into the development process, technologists can create solutions that are not only innovative but also aligned with societal values.

Regulation plays a vital role in guiding the ethical development and use of digital technologies. Governments and international bodies must develop and enforce regulations that address the ethical challenges posed by emerging technologies. This includes setting standards for data privacy, cybersecurity, and the ethical use of AI. However, regulation must be flexible and adaptive to keep pace with the rapid evolution of technology. Collaborative approaches that involve multiple stakeholders, including industry, academia, and civil society, are essential for developing effective regulatory frameworks.

Public engagement and education are crucial for shaping our digital destiny. As digital technologies impact all aspects of life, it is important to involve the public in discussions about their ethical implications. Public consultations, forums, and debates provide platforms for diverse perspectives and help build a broader societal consensus on ethical standards and norms. Promoting digital literacy and education is also vital for empowering individuals to navigate the digital landscape and make informed decisions about their digital lives.

International cooperation is essential for addressing the global nature of digital technologies. Many ethical and regulatory challenges, such as data privacy, cybersecurity, and the regulation of AI, require coordinated international efforts. International organisations, such as the United Nations, the Organisation for Economic Co-operation and Development (OECD), and the World Economic Forum, play key roles in facilitating dialogue and developing global standards and frameworks. Bilateral and multilateral agreements can help align national policies and promote cooperation on shared digital governance challenges.

Innovation and flexibility are key principles for crafting our digital destiny. The rapid pace of technological change means that policies and frameworks must be adaptable and forward-looking. Regulatory sandboxes, which provide controlled environments for testing new technologies and business models, are examples of innovative approaches to regulation that can foster innovation while ensuring adequate oversight. Encouraging responsible innovation involves creating environments where ethical considerations are integral to the development process and where stakeholders are incentivised to prioritise social good.

The intersection of digital technologies and sustainability is another crucial area for consideration. As digital technologies become more integrated into all aspects of society, their environmental impact must be addressed. Sustainable technology practices, such as energy-efficient computing, recycling of electronic waste, and the use of environmentally friendly materials, are essential for reducing the ecological footprint of digital innovations. By aligning technological progress with environmental sustainability, we can ensure that our digital future supports the long-term health and well-being of our planet.

Crafting our digital destiny requires a holistic approach that integrates technological innovation with ethical governance, public engagement, and international cooperation. By addressing the ethical and social implications of digital technologies and prioritising the principles of justice, equity, and human dignity, we can harness the transformative power of technology to create a future that benefits all members of society. This vision of a just and equitable digital future is not only achievable but essential for ensuring that technological progress enhances human well-being and promotes a sustainable and inclusive world.

Charting Our Digital Future: A Call to Ethical Action

As we conclude our exploration of the intricate relationship between technology and ethics, it is clear that the decisions we make today will significantly influence the trajectory of our digital future. This chapter summarises the key points discussed throughout the book and emphasises the imperative of embedding ethical considerations into the future development and use of technology.

The journey began with an introduction to the transformative potential of digital technologies and the pressing need for ethical frameworks to guide their development. We examined the profound impact of artificial intelligence (AI), highlighting the ethical challenges posed by algorithmic bias, transparency, and accountability. Ensuring fairness and equity in AI systems is crucial, requiring rigorous testing, diverse datasets, and explainable models.

Data privacy emerged as another central theme. The proliferation of digital devices and services has led to an unprecedented collection of personal data, raising significant concerns about privacy and security. Robust data protection measures, transparent data practices, and regulations like the General Data Protection Regulation (GDPR) are essential for safeguarding individual privacy and building trust in digital technologies.

We also explored the ethical implications of emerging technologies such as biotechnology, quantum computing, and the Internet of Things (IoT). These technologies hold great promise but also pose complex ethical dilemmas. For instance, gene editing technologies like CRISPR offer the potential to eradicate genetic disorders but raise questions about the limits of human enhancement and equitable access. Quantum computing's vast computational power necessitates new approaches to data security and ethical use.

The role of digital governance and policy was underscored as vital for addressing these ethical challenges. Effective governance frameworks must balance innovation with public interest, ensuring that technology serves humanity's collective well-being. This involves developing adaptive regulatory models, fostering international cooperation, and promoting public engagement and education.

Public engagement and education were highlighted as critical components of ethical digital governance. Empowering individuals with the knowledge and skills to navigate the digital landscape and participate in ethical discussions is essential. This includes integrating digital literacy into educational curricula and facilitating public consultations to reflect diverse perspectives in policy-making.

The environmental impact of technology was another significant concern. Sustainable technology practices, such as energy-efficient computing, e-waste recycling, and the use of eco-friendly materials, are necessary to mitigate the ecological footprint of digital innovations. Aligning technological progress with environmental sustainability is crucial for ensuring the long-term health of our planet.

As we move forward, a collective call to action is imperative. The ethical development and use of technology must be prioritised at all levels, from individual choices to corporate practices and government policies. Here are key actions to consider:

> **Commit to Ethical AI**: Developers and organisations must prioritise fairness, transparency, and accountability in AI systems. This involves continuous monitoring for biases, ensuring explainability, and implementing robust governance frameworks.
>
> **Enhance Data Privacy**: Strengthen data protection measures and uphold individuals' rights to privacy. Adopt transparent data practices and comply with regulations to build trust and protect personal information.
>
> **Promote Digital Inclusion**: Work towards bridging the digital divide by expanding access to digital infrastructure and education. Ensure that technological advancements benefit all segments of society, particularly underserved and marginalised communities.
>
> **Foster Sustainable Practices**: Embrace sustainable technology practices to reduce environmental impact. Design products for longevity and recyclability, and support

initiatives that promote energy efficiency and eco-friendly materials.

Engage in Public Dialogue: Facilitate public engagement and education to foster a culture of ethical awareness. Encourage inclusive dialogue that incorporates diverse perspectives and empowers individuals to participate in shaping the digital future.

Collaborate Internationally: Strengthen international cooperation to address global ethical challenges. Develop harmonised regulatory frameworks and share best practices to promote ethical standards across borders.

The future of technology holds immense potential to enhance human well-being and drive progress. However, realising this potential requires a steadfast commitment to ethical principles. By integrating ethics into every aspect of technology development and use, we can craft a digital destiny that is just, equitable, and sustainable. Let us embrace this responsibility with determination and vision, ensuring that the technologies of tomorrow reflect the values and aspirations of a humane and forward-looking society.

About the Author

Ethan Ray is a thought leader in the realm of digital ethics and a champion for responsible technology use. Building on the success of his first book, "*The Zen of Digital Balance*," Ethan continues to explore the complex relationship between human behaviour and digital innovation in his latest work, "Digital Dilemmas: Navigating Ethics in the Age of AI and Surveillance." With a background in behavioural psychology, Ethan has dedicated his career to understanding how technology impacts our lives and how we can harness its potential while mitigating its risks. His insights into digital ethics and wellness have made him a sought-after speaker and consultant, advising on creating environments that balance productivity, well-being, and ethical integrity. Ethan's work is driven by a passion for fostering a more humane and equitable digital future.

9 789358 810714